TRUSTS, WILLS AND PROBATE LIBRARY

SNELL'S EQUITY

Fifth Supplement
To the Thirty-First Edition

Up-to-date until September 1, 2009

General Editor

JOHN McGHEE Q.C.
M.A. (Oxon.)
of Lincoln's Inn, Barrister

Contributors

MATTHEW CONAGLEN

TIMOTHY DUTTON

DAVID FOX

TIMOTHY HARRY

EDWIN JOHNSON

THOMAS LEECH

SWEET & MAXWELL      **THOMSON REUTERS**

Published in 2009 by
Thomson Reuters (Legal) Limited
(Registered in England and Wales, Company No. 1679046.
Registered Office and address for service:
100 Avenue Road, London, NW3 3PF)
trading as Sweet and Maxwell
For further information on our products and services, visit
www.sweetandmaxwell.co.uk
Typeset by LBJ Typesetting Ltd of Kingsclere
Printed in Great Britain by Athenaeum Press Ltd., Gateshead, Tyne & Wear

No natural forests were destroyed to make this product;
only farmed timber was used and replanted
A CIP catalogue record for this book is available from the British Library
ISBN 978–0–41404–181–3

© 2009 Thomson Reuters (Legal) Limited
Main Work
©
Sweet & Maxwell 2004

NOTE TO READERS

This is the fifth supplement to the text. It takes into account developments up to September 1, 2009. Developments since then are noted on the Snell website, *snellsequity.co.uk* which is updated regularly and is available free of charge.

Contents

PART VII—SECURITIES

TABLE OF CASES

vii

TABLE OF STATUTES

CHAPTER 3

ASSIGNMENT OF CHOSES IN ACTION

1. COMMON LAW AND EQUITY

1. Definition

ADD AT END OF FIRST PARAGRAPH: Not all rights can be regarded as property **3–1** so as to amount to choses in action. Thus in *Goel v Pick* [2006] EWHC 833 (Ch) it was held that a vehicle registration mark did not constitute property and could not be described as a chose in action.

ADD AT END OF FIRST PARAGRAPH: There must however be some outward **3–13** expression by the assignor of his intention to make an immediate disposition of the subject matter of the assignment: *Finlan v Eyton Morris Winfield* [2007] EWHC 914 (Ch).

NOTE 60. ADD: *Coulter v Chief Constable of Dorset Police* was affirmed by the Court of Appeal on other grounds: [2004] EWCA Civ. 1259.

NOTE 40. ADD: See also *Technotrade Ltd v Larkstore Ltd* [2006] EWCA Civ **3–25** 1079; [2006] 42 E.G. 246.

NOTE 47. ADD: See also *Ruttle Plant v Secretary of State* [2008] EWHC 238 **3–44** (TCC).

ADD AT END: Whilst a liquidator may assign a bare cause of action or the fruits of the action, he may not assign his discretionary power to prosecute or carry on proceedings: *Ruttle Plant v Secretary of State* [2008] EWHC 238 (TCC).

NOTE 54. ADD: But notwithstanding the personal nature of a condi- **3–46** tional fee agreement with a solicitor, such an agreement is assignable by one firm to another firm where the solicitor responsible for the matter moves to that other firm: *Jenkins v Young Bros Transport Ltd* [2006] EWHC 151 (QB); [2006] 1 W.L.R. 3189.

NOTE 63. ADD: See also *Barbados Trust Co v Bank of Zambia* [2007] EWCA **3–47** Civ 148; [2007] 1 Lloyd's Rep 495.

CHAPTER 5

THE MAXIMS OF EQUITY

6. HE WHO COMES INTO EQUITY MUST COME WITH CLEAN HANDS

NOTE 43. ADD: Cf. *Barrett v Barrett* [2008] EWHC 1061 (Ch).   **5–15**

7. DELAY DEFEATS EQUITIES, OR, EQUITY AIDS THE VIGILANT AND NOT
   THE INDOLENT: VIGILANTIBUS, NON DORMENTIBUS JURA SUBVENIUNT

DELETE AND REPLACE SECOND PARAGRAPH AS FOLLOWS: **5–16**
There are three cases to consider:

(a) equitable claims to which the Statute applies expressly;
(b) equitable claims to which the Statute is applied by analogy; and
(c) equitable claims to which no statute applies and which are
    therefore covered by the ordinary rules of laches.

Although the doctrine of laches applies principally to claims to which
the Statute does not apply either directly or by analogy, it is important
to note that the doctrine of laches is capable of applying in these cases
too at least where there has been unjustied delay coupled with an
adverse effect of some kind on the defendant or a third party: *P&O
Nedlloyd B.V. v Arab Metals Co. [2006] EWCA Civ 1717.*

ADD AT END OF FIRST PARAGRAPH: However the Statute will not be **5–18**
applied to a claim for specific performance of a contract since such a
claim does not depend on proving any breach of contract: *P & O
Nedlloyd BV v Arab Metals Co* [2006] EWCA Civ 1717.

DELETE SECOND PARAGRAPH

NOTE 69. ADD: The test set out in *Frawley v Neill* [2000] C.P. Rep 20 was **5–19**
applied by the Court of Appeal in *Patel v Shah* [2005] EWCA Civ 157.

ADD AFTER SECOND SENTENCE OF LAST PARAGRAPH: They can even include a
claim by a beneficiary against trustees for the recovery of trust property,
although the circumstances in which laches will bar such relief otherwise than where the the trust has arisen in the course of a commercial

3

relationship are extremely rare: *Patel v Shah* [2005] EWCA Civ 157. See also *Re Loftus (deceased)* [2006] EWCA Civ 1124; [2007] 1 W.L.R. 591.

Chapter 6

THE EQUITABLE DOCTRINES

Election

1. The doctrine of election

NOTE 58. ADD: See also *Nexus Communications Group Ltd v Lambert* [2005] **6–16** EWHC 345 where it was said that the doctrine means that a person cannot accept the benefit under any instrument or judgment without taking the accompanying burden and, by analogy, extends so as to prevent a person who has obtained judgment on the basis of a particular contention from resisting judgment based on an inconsistent contention where it would be inequitable to do so.

AMEND LAST SENTENCE SO AS TO READ: Subject to the power to receive **6–31** extrinsic evidence pursuant to the provisions of section 21 of the Administration of Justice Act 1982 [fn4a], parol evidence is not admissible to show that the testator intended to include property which he wrongly thought to be his own in a general devise or bequest [fn 5].

ADD NEW NOTE 4A: *Frear v Frear* [2008] EWCA Civ 1320.

CHAPTER 7

FIDUCIARIES

FIDUCIARIES AND FIDUCIARY RELATIONSHIPS

1. "Fiduciary"

NOTE 3. ADD: *South Australia v Peat Marwick Mitchell & Co* (1997) 24 **7–2**
A.C.S.R. 231, 266.

END OF PARAGRAPH: Add new footnote: SEE *Chirnside v Fay* [2006] NZSC **7–4**
68 at [72].

ADD AT END OF PARAGRAPH: *Directors*: Once in force, the Companies Act **7–6**
2006 provides a statutory code of duties for directors, in place of the
common law and equitable duties to which directors have hitherto been
subject: see s.170(3) of the Act. The result is that directors will no longer
be subject to the duties discussed in this chapter, other than insofar as
the 2006 Act so provides. Cases regarding directors which were decided
prior to the implementation of the 2006 Act are clearly still relevant in
this chapter insofar as they state principles which are of application to
fiduciaries generally. Indeed, the 2006 Act provides that such cases are
also relevant in interpreting the provisions of that Act: s.170(4).
However, caution must be exercised with cases decided after the 2006
Act comes into force before dicta in those cases are treated as statements
of principles which apply to fiduciaries generally. The civil consequences of directors acting in breach of the duties contained in the
2006 Act will remain the same as if the corresponding common law or
equitable duties had been breached: s.178(1), Companies Act 2006.

NOTE 11. ADD: *Paper Reclaim Ltd v Aotearoa International Ltd* [2007]
NZSC 26 at [33].

NOTE 13. ADD: *Aequitas v AEFC* [2001] NSWSC 14, (2001) 19 A.C.L.C.
1,006 at [343].

NOTE 14. ADD: *Re Canadian Land Reclaiming & Colonizing Co* (1880) 14
ChD 660, 670 & 673 (CA); *Primlake Ltd (in liq) v Matthews Associates*
[2006] EWHC 1227 (Ch) at [284]; *Shepherds Investments Ltd v Walters*
[2006] EWHC 836 (Ch) at [78].

ADD AFTER NOTE 15: nor generally shadow directors: *Ultraframe (UK)
Ltd v Fielding* [2005] EWHC 1638 (Ch) at [1284], [1289], although see now
s.170(5), Companies Act 2006.

NOTE 16. ADD: *Nant-y-glo & Blaina Ironworks Co v Grave* (1878) 12 ChD 738; *Eden v Ridsdales Railway Lamp & Lighting Co Ltd* (1889) 23 QBD 368.

NOTE 17. ADD: *Glandon Pty Ltd v Strata Consolidated Pty Ltd* (1993) 11 A.C.S.R. 543 at 547 (NSWCA).

7-7   NOTE 23. ADD: *Tate v Williamson* (1866) L.R. 2 Ch. App. 55 at 61(LC); *Waxman v Waxman* (2004) 7 I.T.E.L.R. 162 at [504] (Ont CA); *South Australia v Peat Marwick Mitchell & Co* (1997) 24 A.C.S.R. 231, 264; *Schipp v Cameron* [1998] NSWSC 997 at [695].

NOTE 26. ADD: This paragraph was quoted in *Ultraframe (UK) Ltd v Fielding* [2005] EWHC 1638 (Ch) at [1285].

7-8   NOTE 27. ADD: *Button v Phelps* [2006] EWHC 53 (Ch) at [58]–[61]; *Brooker v Friend* [2006] NSWCA 385 at [149]; *Australian Securities and Investments Commission v Citigroup Global Markets Australia Pty Ltd (ACN 113 114 832) (No. 4)* [2007] F.C.A. 963 at [272]; *South Australia v Peat Marwick Mitchell & Co* (1997) 24 A.C.S.R. 231, 265; *Schipp v Cameron* [1998] NSWSC 997 at [697].

NOTE 28. DELETE: "Youdan (ed.) 1 at 54" and replace with: "Youdan (ed.), *Equity, Fiduciaries and Trusts* (1989) 1 at 54". Add: See also *Waxman v Waxman* (2004) 7 I.T.E.L.R. 162 at [512] (Ont CA); *Brandeis (Brokers) Ltd v Black* [2001] 2 All E.R. (Comm.) 980 at [36]–[37]; *Hughes Aircraft Systems International v Airservices Australia* (1997) 146 A.L.R. 1 at 81 (FCA); *News Ltd v Australian Rugby Football League Ltd* (1996) 64 F.C.R. 410, 541; *Australian Securities Commission v AS Nominees Ltd* (1995) 133 A.L.R. 1 at 17 (F.C.A.); *Glandon Pty Ltd v Strata Consolidated Pty Ltd* (1993) 11 A.C.S.R. 543 at 557 (NSWCA); *Australian Securities and Investments Commission v Citigroup Global Markets Australia Pty Ltd (ACN 113 114 832) (No. 4)* [2007] F.C.A. 963 at [273]. This expectation is assessed objectively, and so it is not necessary for the principal subjectively to harbour the expectation: *South Australia v Peat Marwick Mitchell & Co* (1997) 24 A.C.S.R. 231, 265.

7-9   NOTE 31. ADD: *Commonwealth Bank of Australia v Finding* [2001] 1 Qd. R. 168 at [9]–[10] (CA); *Foley v Hill* (1848) 2 H.L.C. 28 at 36 & 43 (9 E.R. 1002 at 1005 & 1008).

7-10   NOTE 38. ADD: *Chirnside v Fay* [2006] NZSC 68; *Schipp v Cameron* [1998] NSWSC 997; *Fraser Edmiston Pty Ltd v AGT (Qld) Pty Ltd* [1988] 2 Qd. R. 1.

NOTE 39. ADD: *Button v Phelps* [2006] EWHC 53 (Ch) at [59]–[61]; *Ross River Ltd v Cambridge City Football Club Ltd* [2007] EWHC 2115 (Ch) at [197]; *Gibson Motorsport Merchandise Pty Ltd v Forbes* [2006] FCAFC 44 at [2], (2006) 149 F.C.R. 569; and see *Explora Group plc v Hesco Bastion Ltd* [2005] EWCA Civ 646 at [51], citing this paragraph. The New Zealand Supreme Court has recently suggested that joint ventures may be "inherently fiduciary" because of their similarity to partnership: *Chirnside v Fay* [2006] NZSC 68 at [14] & [74] (see also, apparently, *Concrete Pty Ltd v Parramatta Design & Developments Pty Ltd* [2006] HCA 55, (2006) 231 A.L.R. 663 at [156] *per* Callinan J). Given the lack of a clear definition of 'joint venture', this approach creates a risk that many commercial transactions would be treated as fiduciary relationships in circumstances where fiduciary duties would be unnecessary and inappropriate. The problem stems from the fact that the term 'joint venture' is "a term which does not have a precise legal meaning": *BBC Worldwide Ltd v Bee Load Ltd* [2007] EWHC 134 (Comm) at [103]. It is not sensible to use an ill-defined concept as the trigger for the very strict fiduciary duties that arise where a fiduciary relationship is identified. It will be preferable in England to maintain the traditional approach whereby joint ventures are not treated as a settled category of fiduciary relationship, but an individual joint venture may appropriately be treated as a fiduciary relationship if, "after a meticulous examination of its own facts" (*Cook v Evatt (No 2)* [1992] 1 N.Z.L.R. 676, 685; *Foster Bryant Surveying Ltd v Bryant* [2007] EWCA Civ 200 at [76]), the fiduciary expectation mentioned in para.[7–08] is found to be appropriate, bearing in mind the points made in para.[7–11] below regarding the appropriateness of that expectation between commercial actors. This latter suggestion appears now to have been accepted by the New Zealand Supreme Court, which has accepted that joint ventures are not necessarily fiduciary (and, indeed, the label 'joint venture' can be unhelpful in this context) and that a close examination of the contractual matrix is necessary before fiduciary duties can be found: *Paper Reclaim Ltd v Aotearoa Ltd* [2007] NZSC 26 at [31]–[32]; *Maruha Corp v Amaltal Corp Ltd* [2007] NZSC 40 at [20]–[21]. "It is perfectly common for commercial entities to want to enter into cooperative arrangements for a specific purpose, involving a share of profits, but without intending to follow the route of mutual agency and the court should give effect to their intentions": *BBC Worldwide Ltd v Bee Load Ltd* [2007] EWHC 134 (Comm) at [107]. Where the intention is found to be to create some form of agency within a 'joint venture', there can nonetheless be fiduciary duties as to that part of the arrangement between the venturers, while the arrangement is not fiduciary in general: *Maruha Corp v Amaltal Corp Ltd* [2007] NZSC 40 at [21]–[22].

AT END OF PARAGRAPH. ADD: But financial advisers can occupy a fiduciary position vis-a-vis their clients: *Daly v Sydney Stock Exchange Ltd* (1986) 160 C.L.R. 371 at 377; *Aequitas v AEFC* [2001] NSWSC 14, (2001) 19 A.C.L.C. 1,006 at [307].

NOTE 44. ADD: *News Ltd v Australian Rugby Football League Ltd* (1996) 64 **7–11** F.C.R. 410, 538–539; *South Australia v Peat Marwick Mitchell & Co* (1997) 24 A.C.S.R. 231, 266.

GENERAL NATURE OF FIDUCIARY DUTIES

1. Duties of Loyalty

NOTE 49. ADD: *KLB v British Columbia* [2003] 2 S.C.R. 403; (2003) 230 **7–13** D.L.R. (4th) 513 at [48]; *Chirnside v Fay* [2004] 3 N.Z.L.R. 637 at [51]; *Sinclair Investment Holdings SA v Versailles Trade Finance Ltd* [2005]

EWCA Civ 722 at [20]; *Ultraframe (UK) Ltd v Fielding* [2005] EWHC 1638 (Ch) at [1285]–[1288]; *Gibson Motorsport Merchandise Pty Ltd v Forbes* [2006] FCAFC 44 at [11], (2006) 149 F.C.R. 569; *Stevens v Premium Real Estate Ltd* [2009] NZSC 15 at [67].

7–14   END OF FIRST SENTENCE: ADD NOTE 52A: *Australian Securities and Investments Commission v Citigroup Global Markets Australia Pty Ltd (ACN 113 114 832) (No. 4)* [2007] F.C.A. 963 at [291]; *South Australia v Peat Marwick Mitchell & Co* (1997) 24 A.C.S.R. 231, 264.

NOTE 55. ADD: *Ratiu v Conway* [2005] EWCA Civ 1302 at [59]; *Huntington Copper & Sulphur Co (Ltd) v Henderson* (1877) 4 S.C. (4th Series) 294 at 299.

NOTE 58. ADD: The two principles largely overlap but there may be cases where the two do not necessarily both apply: *Oceanic Life Ltd v HIH Casualty & General Insurance Ltd* [1999] NSWSC 292 at [42].

7–15   NOTE 59. ADD: *Ultraframe (UK) Ltd v Fielding* [2005] EWHC 1638 (Ch) at [1305]–[1306]; *John Taylors v Masons* [2001] EWCA Civ 2106 at [20]–[28], [2005] W.T.L.R. 1519.

NOTE 60. ADD: See also *Ross River Ltd v Cambridge City Football Club Ltd* [2007] EWHC 2115 (Ch) at [250], mentioning the "propensity" for misconduct that a bribe creates.

7–17   NOTE 61. ADD: *Roberts v R* [2002] 4 S.C.R. 245; (2002) 220 D.L.R. (4th) 1 at [83]; *Chirnside v Fay* [2004] 3 N.Z.L.R. 637 at [51] "it is not the function of fiduciary law to mediate between the various interests of parties who are dealing with each other. That is for contract law. Fiduciary law serves to support the integrity and utility of relationships in which the role of one party is perceived to be the service of the interests of the other. It does so by imposing a specific duty of loyalty."

NOTE 62. ADD: *Ratiu v Conway* [2005] EWCA Civ 1302 at [71]–[72]; *Strother v 3464920 Canada Inc* [2007] S.C.C. 24 at [141].

ADD AT END OF PARAGRAPH: "not every breach of duty by a fiduciary is a breach of fiduciary duty": *Hilton v Barker Booth & Eastwood* [2005] UKHL 8; [2005] 1 W.L.R. 567 at [29]; *Bristol & West Building Society v Mothew* [1998] Ch. 1 at 16; *Base Metal Trading Ltd v Shamurin* [2004] EWCA Civ 1316; [2005] 1 All E.R. (Comm.) 17 at [19]; *Chirnside v Fay* [2006] NZSC 68 at [15], [72] & [73]; *Strother v 3464920 Canada Inc* [2007] SCC 24 at [34]; *South Australia v Peat Marwick Mitchell & Co* (1997) 24 A.C.S.R. 231, 266.

7–19   NOTE 69. ADD: *Aequitas v AEFC* [2001] NSWSC 14, (2001) 19 A.C.L.C. 1,006 at [284]; *Australian Securities and Investments Commission v Citigroup Global Markets Australia Pty Ltd (ACN 113 114 832) (No. 4)* [2007] F.C.A. 963 at [290]; *Brooker v Friend* [2006] NSWCA 385 at [26]; *Gibson Motorsport Merchandise Pty Ltd v Forbes* [2006] FCAFC 44 at [12], (2006) 149 F.C.R. 569.

7–20   NOTE 70. ADD: *Strother v 3464920 Canada Inc* [2007] S.C.C. 24 at [118] & [141]; *Australian Securities and Investments Commission v Citigroup Global*

Markets Australia Pty Ltd (ACN 113 114 832) (No. 4) [2007] F.C.A. 963 at [288]; *South Australia v Peat Marwick Mitchell & Co* (1997) 24 A.C.S.R. 231, 266; *Stevens v Premium Real Estate Ltd* [2009] NZSC 15 at [23].

NOTE 72. ADD: *Brooker v Friend* [2006] NSWCA 385 at [26]. For an example of the importance of defining the fiduciary's *non*-fiduciary duties, see the difference of opinion between the majority and the dissent in *Strother v 3464920 Canada Inc* [2007] S.C.C. 24, which was focused on the content of the lawyer's contractual retainer. Also, in *Australian Securities and Investments Commission v Citigroup Global Markets Australia Pty Ltd (ACN 113 114 832) (No. 4)* [2007] F.C.A. 963, an investment bank was held not to occupy a fiduciary position vis-a-vis its client as a result of a contractual exclusion of any such relationship: see, especially, at [324]–[335].

ADD AT END OF PARAGRAPH: Where the fiduciary's duty is owed to a company, courts are more prepared to look behind the corporate veil to identify the persons to whom, as a matter of practical and common-sense reality, the fiduciary's duties are owed: *Ratiu v Conway* [2005] EWCA Civ 1302 at [78]–[80], [186] & [188].

NOTE 73. ADD: *Australian Securities and Investments Commission v Citigroup Global Markets Australia Pty Ltd (ACN 113 114 832) (No. 4)* [2007] FCA 963 at [285]. Such an inference can be drawn either from the inherent nature of the type of relationship (as in *Kelly v Cooper*) or from the particular facts of the individual relationship: see *ASIC v Citigroup* at [355]–[360]. **7–21**

NOTE 74. ADD: *Foster Bryant Surveying Ltd v Bryant* [2007] EWCA Civ 200 at [8] & [68]. The fact that fiduciary duties do not apply after the retainer has been does not mean other doctrines, such as breach of confidence, are inapplicable: see *Bolkiah v KPMG*. Further, the court may be able to intervene where a solicitor acts against a former client, in the exercise of its inherent jurisdiction to over solicitors as officers of the court, although it should be slow to do so: *Winters v Mishcon de Reya* [2008] EWHC 2419 (Ch) at [94]. **7–22**

NOTE 77. ADD: *Edmonds v Donovan* [2005] V.S.C.A. 27 at [56]–[57] & [60]–[61]. **7–23**

ADD AT END OF PARAGRAPH: Thus, a director who resigns does not avoid liability under the profit rule "if, after his resignation, he uses for his own benefit property of the company or information which he has acquired while a director": *Ultraframe (UK) Ltd v Fielding* [2005] EWHC 1638 (Ch) at [1309].

NOTE 82. ADD: See also *Foster Bryant Surveying Ltd v Bryant* [2007] EWCA Civ 200. **7–24**

ADD AT END OF PARAGRAPH: After October 2008 (when the Companies Act 2006 comes into force), company directors cannot avoid liability by resigning in respect of (a) his duty under s.175 of the Act to avoid conflicts of interest as regards the exploitation of any property, information or opportunity of which he became aware while he was a director; and (b) his duty under s.176 not to accept benefits from third parties as regards things done or omitted by him while a director: see s.170(2), Companies Act 2006.

CONFLICTS BETWEEN DUTY AND INTEREST

General principle

7–25 ADD AT END OF PARAGRAPH: For company directors, see now s.175, Companies Act 2006, which stands in place of the pre-existing rules on conflicts between duty and interest.

NOTE 86: *Ultraframe (UK) Ltd v Fielding* [2005] EWHC 1638 (Ch) at [1308]–[1310] & [1330].

7–26 NOTE 89. ADD: *Australian Securities and Investments Commission v Citigroup Global Markets Australia Pty Ltd (ACN 113 114 832) (No. 4)* [2007] F.C.A. 963 at [313].

NOTE 90. ADD: *Eden v Ridsdales Railway Lamp & Lighting Co Ltd* (1889) 23 QBD 368, 371 (CA).

7–31 NOTE 6. ADD: *Australian Securities and Investments Commission v Citigroup Global Markets Australia Pty Ltd (ACN 113 114 832) (No. 4)* [2007] F.C.A. 963 at [278]–[280].

NOTE 8. ADD: "A person occupying a fiduciary position will be absolved from liability for what would otherwise be a breach of duty by obtaining a fully informed consent": *Australian Securities and Investments Commission v Citigroup Global Markets Australia Pty Ltd (ACN 113 114 832) (No. 4)* [2007] F.C.A. 963 at [293].

ADD AT END OF PARAGRAPH: For company directors, see now s.175(4)–(6) and s.180, Companies Act 2006, which stands in place of the pre-existing rules.

2. Authorisation

7–32 NOTE 17. ADD: *Gwembe Valley Development Co Ltd v Koshy* [2003] EWCA Civ 1478; [2004] 1 B.C.L.C. 131 at [65]; *Wrexham Association Football Club Ltd v Crucialmove Ltd* [2006] EWCA Civ 237, [2007] B.C.C. 139 at [39].

NOTE 21. ADD: *Strother v 3464920 Canada Inc* [2007] SCC 24 at [55]; *Australian Securities and Investments Commission v Citigroup Global Markets Australia Pty Ltd (ACN 113 114 832) (No. 4)* [2007] F.C.A. 963 at [295].

ADD AT END OF LAST SENTENCE: Disclosure is treated in a functional, rather than a formalistic, way, so that the sufficiency of disclosure may depend on the sophistication and intelligence of the person to whom disclosure is required to be made: *Farah Constructions Pty Ltd v Say-Dee*

Pty Ltd [2007] H.C.A. 22 at [107]–[108]; *Australian Securities and Invest-ments Commission v Citigroup Global Markets Australia Pty Ltd (ACN 113 114 832) (No. 4)* [2007] F.C.A. 963 at [296]; both of the preceding cases involve sophisticated principals: *cf.* the facts in *Maguire v Makaronis* (1997) 188 C.L.R. 449.

ADD AT END OF LAST SENTENCE: . . . and fiduciaries will not be heard to **7–33** say that they were unaware of their personal interest where it was their professional duty to be aware of such interests: *Segrave v Kirwan* (1828) Beatty 157; *Bulkley v Wilford* (1834) 2 Cl. & Fin. 102, 177, 181 & 183 (HL); *Bayly v Wilkins* (1846) 3 Jones & La Touche 630, 635.

NOTE 32. ADD: Company Directors can also seek relief from liability **7–35** under s.727 of the Companies Act 1985: see, *eg, PNC Telecom plc v Thomas (No 2)* [2007] EWHC 2157 (Ch) at [43] & [91]–[105], [2008] 2 B.C.L.C. 95; *Green v Walkling* [2007] EWHC 3251 (Ch) at [42]–[51], [2008] 2 B.C.L.C. 332. See now s 1157, Companies Act 2006.

3. Application

END OF SECOND SENTENCE. ADD: NOTE 35A : *Huntington Copper & Sulphur Co* **7–36** *(Ltd) v Henderson* (1877) 4 S.C. (4th Series) 294 at 299.

NOTE 43. ADD: *Newgate Stud Co v Penfold* [2004] EWHC 2993 (Ch) at **7–37** [222].

NOTE 49. ADD: *Newgate Stud Co v Penfold* [2004] EWHC 2993 (Ch) at **7–38** [230].

ADD AT END OF PARAGRAPH: A transaction between a fiduciary and his **7–39** wife must be shown to have been in the best interests of the fiduciary's principal in order to be upheld: *Newgate Stud Co v Penfold* [2004] EWHC 2993 (Ch) at [234]–[244]. Even this may not be necessary if the circum-stances of the case are such that the wife ought to be identified as her husband—"there are wives and there are wives": *Tito v Waddell (No 2)* [1977] Ch 106, 240.

ADD AT END OF PARAGRAPH: For company directors, see now s.177 and s.182, Companies Act 2006, which stands in place of the pre-existing rules on transactions between a director and his company (see also s.175(3), excluding application of that Act's general statutory prohibition on conflicts between duty and interest).

ADD NEW FOOTNOTE AT END OF FIRST SENTENCE: e.g., *HSBC International* **7–76** *Trustee Ltd v Tam Mei Kam* (2004) 7 I.T.E.L.R. 382 (HK HC).

4. CONFLICTS BETWEEN DUTY AND DUTY

2. Application

NOTE 99. ADD: *Waxman v Waxman* (2004) 7 I.T.E.L.R. 162 at [646] (Ont **7–91** CA).

7–93   note 4: *Ultraframe (UK) Ltd v Fielding* [2005] EWHC 1638 (Ch) at [1317].

7–98   note 18. add: *Hilton v Barker Booth & Eastwood* [2005] UKHL 8; [2005] 1 W.L.R. 567 at [35], [38], [41] & [44].

5. Profits Made out of Fiduciary Position

1. General Principle

7–99   add at end of second sentence: or otherwise within the scope of that fiduciary office: *United Pan-Europe Communications NV v Deutsche Bank AG* [2000] 2 B.C.L.C. 461 at [47]; *Murad v Al-Saraj* [2005] EWCA Civ 959 at [112].

7–100   add at end of first sentence: "and will apply even where the fiduciary is free of any moral blame": *Halton International Inc (Holding) SARL v Guernroy Ltd* [2005] EWHC 1968 (Ch) at [141]. "The rule is not dependent on fraud or bad faith or whether the actions of the fiduciary were clandestine. The rule is dependent on the mere fact of the profit being made": *John Taylors v Masons* [2001] EWCA Civ 2106 at [46], [2005] W.T.L.R. 1519.

note 25. add: *Foster Bryant Surveying Ltd v Bryant* [2007] EWCA Civ 200 at [88] & [101].

add at end of paragraph: It has recently been suggested that the rule might be tempered in circumstances where it operates harshly on a fiduciary, such as where the fiduciary acted in perfect good faith and without any deception or concealment and in the belief that he was acting in the best interests of the principal, or where the profit taken was one which the principal would never have opted to take for himself: see *Murad v Al-Saraj* [2005] EWCA Civ 959 at [82]–[83], [121] & [158]; *John Taylors v Masons* [2001] EWCA Civ 2106 at [41], [2005] W.T.L.R. 1519, although *cf.* at [44] . However, that does not currently represent the law, and would require a decision of the House of Lords given the high authority indicating the contrary: *Murad v Al-Saraj*, above at [83] & [121]–[122]; *John Taylors v Masons* [2001] EWCA Civ 2106 at [46], [2005] W.T.L.R. 1519; *Wrexham Association Football Club Ltd v Crucialmove Ltd* [2006] EWCA Civ 237 at [51].

7–101   add at end of paragraph: For company directors, see now s.176, Companies Act 2006, which stands in place of the pre-existing rules on unauthorised profits made out of a fiduciary position.

2. Authorisation

7–102   note 30. add: *John Taylors v Masons* [2001] EWCA Civ 2106 at [45], [2005] W.T.L.R. 1519.

note 31. add: *Ultraframe (UK) Ltd v Fielding* [2005] EWHC 1638 (Ch) at [1318].

3. Application

NOTE 35. ADD: *Blythe v Northwood* [2005] NSWCA 221 at [196]–[197]. **7–105**

NOTE 36. ADD: See similarly: *John Taylors v Masons* [2001] EWCA Civ 2106, [2005] W.T.L.R. 1519 (regarding a new licence obtained by former partners).

NOTE 61. ADD: *Aequitas v AEFC* [2001] NSWSC 14, (2001) 19 A.C.L.C. **7–110** 1,006 at [370]; *Wilson v Hurstanger Ltd* [2007] EWCA Civ 299 at [34]; *Ross River Ltd v Cambridge City Football Club Ltd* [2007] EWHC 2115 (Ch) at [203]–[204] & [218].

NOTE 65. ADD: *Ross River Ltd v Cambridge City Football Club Ltd* [2007] EWHC 2115 (Ch) at [218].

NOTE 66. ADD: *Ross River Ltd v Cambridge City Football Club Ltd* [2007] EWHC 2115 (Ch) at [205] & [218].

ADD TO FOOTNOTE 71: The rationale underlying this rule must be that **7–111** the trustee cannot be held liable where there is no risk whatsoever that the trustee could have been influenced inconsistently with his duty, as where the trustee received profits other than as a result of his or her own volition. The strict rule ought to be applied if there is any element of volition on the part of the trustee, in order to excise any risk of temptation.

ADD TO NOTE 76: Not all sub-agency arrangements involve fiduciary **7–113** duties owed by the sub-agent to the originating principal: see, eg, *New Zealand & Australian Land Co v Watson* (1881) 7 Q.B.D. 374 (CA).

NOTE 82: *Ultraframe (UK) Ltd v Fielding* [2005] EWHC 1638 (Ch) at **7–116** [1355]; *John Taylors v Masons* [2001] EWCA Civ 2106 at [34], [2005] W.T.L.R. 1519.

ADD AT END OF PARAGRAPH: After October 2008, the "corporate opportunity" application of the fiduciary conflict and profit rules will be displaced by the provisions contained in the Companies Act 2006, especially ss.175 and 176.

ADD AT END OF PARAGRAPH: Similarly, where a pre-existing contract **7–117** between a partnership and its client was renewed in favour of one partner alone, the succeeding contract was treated as having been renewed because of the partner's fiduciary position, in the absence of evidence to the contrary: *Lindsley v Woodfull* [2004] EWCA Civ 165; [2004] 2 B.C.L.C. 131 at [28].

ADD AT END OF PARAGRAPH: A director was recently held liable for non- **7–119** disclosure of his own misconduct, although the Court of Appeal rejected the notion that there was a separate and independent fiduciary duty to disclose such misconduct: *Fassihi v Item Software (UK) Ltd* [2004] EWCA Civ 1244 at [41]. It remains unclear whether the director's obligation in this case was a fiduciary obligation: it was justified on the basis of the fiduciary position held, and the duty of loyalty owed, by directors (at [34], [41]) although the duty appears capable of being owed also by employees (at [55], [60]), raising the question whether it is a duty "peculiar to fiduciaries" (see *Bristol & West Building Society v Mothew* [1998] Ch. 1 at 16); see also *Shepherds Investments Ltd v Walters* [2006] EWHC 836 (Ch) at [132]. The justification given in Shepherds Investments v Walters is more orthodox: a director is in breach of fiduciary duty if he acts with a conflict between duty and interest (including where he is personally competing with the company) without disclosing that to the company and seeking consent. However, Etherton J. also considered it a breach of fiduciary duty for the director to fail to disclose any information which is of relevance and concern to the company, which does not appear to require any conflict between duty and interest and which is a positive duty. Australian courts have rejected the decision in Fassihi as inconsistent with the proscriptive nature of fiduciary duties: *P & V Industries Pty Ltd v Porto* [2006] V.S.C. 131 at [32]–[34], [43]. The duty of disclosure can be understood instead as a part of the director's general (company law) duty to act in good faith in the best interests of the company. In *Helmet Integrated Systems Ltd v Tunnard* [2006] EWCA Civ 1735 an employee was held not to have acted in breach of fiduciary duties when he took preparatory steps toward developing a competing business, despite the fact that those preparatory steps had not been disclosed to his employer. Some of the confusion contained in (and created by) these cases ought to abate as the provisions of the Companies Act 2006 come into force creating a code of directors' duties. However, that will not avoid the issue completely as there will remain cases where the person concerned is not a director but is nonetheless held to owe fiduciary duties (e.g., some non-directorial employees).

6. REMEDIES FOR BREACH OF FIDUCIARY DUTY

1. Recission

7–121   NOTE 3. DELETE "[1988] 1 W.L.R. 156" and replace with "[1988] 1 W.L.R. 1256"

7–126   ADD AT END OF PARAGRAPH: The principal is entitled to rescind if he neither knew of, nor consented to, a payment made to his fiduciary in breach of fiduciary duty: *Ross River Ltd v Cambridge City Football Club Ltd* [2007] EWHC 2115 (Ch) at [203]. Where the principal is aware that his fiduciary has been paid a commission by the other party to the transaction but there has been insufficient disclosure for the principal to have given a fully informed consent (e.g., indicating the amount of the commission and making clear that the principal's consent was being sought), the court has a discretion as to whether to order rescission. The court has refused to order rescission in such a situation where it considered that the agreement was fair and enforceable: *Wilson v*

Hurstanger Ltd [2007] EWCA Civ 299 at [43]–[51] (see also *Ross River Ltd v Cambridge City Football Club Ltd* [2007] EWHC 2115 (Ch) at [203]).

2. Account of profits

NOTE 23. ADD: *East India Co v Henchman* (1791) 1 Ves. Jun. 287 at 289 (30   **7–127**
E.R. 347 at 348); *Wilson v Hurstanger Ltd* [2007] EWCA Civ 299 at [35].

ADD AT END OF PARAGRAPH: Considerations of causation, such as those relevant to claims for common law damages, are not relevant (*United Pan-Europe Communications NV v Deutsche Bank AG* [2000] 2 B.C.L.C. 461 at [47]), but there must be a link between the profits in respect of which an account is sought and the fiduciary position or breach of fiduciary duty complained of: *Button v Phelps* [2006] EWHC 53 (Ch) at [66]; *Murad v Al-Saraj* [2005] EWCA Civ 959 at [85], [112] & [115]–[116], [2005] W.T.L.R. 1573; *Chirnside v Fay* [2006] NZSC 68 at [36]; *Strother v 3464920 Canada Inc* [2007] S.C.C. 24 at [79] & [89]–[95]. Further, an account of profits can be rendered inappropriate where the claimant stands by for a length period before seeking the remedy, such that it is exposed to none of the risks involved but seeks all of the rewards and despite knowing about the breach: *Edmonds v Donovan* [2005] V.S.C.A. 27 at [77].

NOTE 25. ADD: *Ultraframe (UK) Ltd v Fielding* [2005] EWHC 1638 (Ch) at   **7–129**
[1579].

ADD AFTER NOTE 25: The governing principles are that the fiduciary must account for all of his unauthorised profit, but this accounting must not be allowed to operate so as to unjustly enrich the claimant and so the profits for which the fiduciary must account must bear some reasonable relationship to the breach of fiduciary duty: *Ultraframe (UK) Ltd v Fielding* [2005] EWHC 1638 (Ch) at [1588]; see also *Strother v 3464920 Canada Inc* [2007] S.C.C. 24 at [74] (equitable remedies discretionary).

ADD AT END OF PARAGRAPH: The account of profits strips the fiduciary's profit and as such, is a quite distinct remedy from the remedy which forces the fiduciary to compensate the claimant for its loss: the fact that the fiduciary can show that the claimant would not have made a loss had there been no breach of fiduciary duty is therefore irrelevant so far as an account of profits is concerned: *Murad v Al-Saraj* [2005] EWCA Civ 959 at [67] & [136]; *Gray v New Augarita Porcupine Mines Ltd* [1952] 3 D.L.R. 1, 15. Only actual consent can obviate this liability: *Murad v Al-Saraj* [2005] EWCA Civ 959 at [71].

NOTE 29. ADD: For an example of directions given as to accounts where   **7–130**
a licence was obtained in breach of fiduciary duties owed to former partners, see, e.g., *John Taylors v Masons* [2001] EWCA Civ 2106 at [37], [2005] W.T.L.R. 1519.

ADD AT END OF PARAGRAPH: This is based on the understanding that, "given the property in question is the goodwill of the company's business, there will in all probability come a time when it can safely be said that any future profits of the new business will be attributable not to the goodwill misappropriated from the claimant company when the new business was set up but rather to the defendants' own efforts in carrying on that business": *Murad v Al-Saraj* [2005] EWCA Civ 959 at [115].

However, a fiduciary does not automatically avoid the obligation to account entirely for a profit made in breach of fiduciary duty by arranging for the profit to be earned through a separate corporate entity: see, e.g., *Lindsley v Woodfull* [2004] EWCA Civ 165; [2004] 2 B.C.L.C. 131 at [27]–[28]; *Quarter Master UK Ltd v Pyke* [2004] EWHC 1815 (Ch); [2005] 1 BCLC 245 at [75]; *CMS Dolphin Ltd v Simonet* [2001] 2 B.C.L.C. 704 at [100]–[103]; *Cook v Deeks* [1916] A.C. 554. The fiduciary bears the onus of convincing the court that an account of the entire profits is inequitable in all the circumstances: *Warman International Ltd v Dwyer* (1995) 182 C.L.R. 544 at 561–562. The corporate veil will be pierced where a fiduciary has used a corporate vehicle as a device or facade to conceal the true facts (*Trustor AB v Smallbone (No. 2)* [2001] 1 W.L.R. 1177 at [23]; *Sinclair Investment Holdings SA v Versailles Trade Finance Ltd* [2007] EWHC 915 (Ch) at [104]) and where the company is a mere cloak or alter ego of the fiduciary (*Gencor ACP Ltd v Dalby* [2000] 2 B.C.L.C. 734, 744; *Sinclair Investment Holdings SA v Versailles Trade Finance Ltd* [2007] EWHC 915 (Ch) at [104]), but not merely where the fiduciary has a substantial interest in a company: *Ultraframe (UK) Ltd v Fielding* [2005] EWHC 1638 (Ch) at [1576].

7–131   NOTE 31. ADD: *Lindsley v Woodfull* [2004] EWCA Civ 720; [2004] 2 B.C.L.C. 131 at [6] & [8]; *Re Macadam* [1946] Ch. 73, 82–83; *Cook v Collingridge* (1823) Jac. 607, 623; *Brown v de Tastet* (1821) Jac. 284, 294, 298 & 299. Indeed, such allowances can even be appropriate where a constructive trust is awarded: *Fraser Edmiston Pty Ltd v AGT (Qld) Pty Ltd* [1988] 2 Qd. R. 1, 12.

NOTE 33. ADD: Contrary to what Campbell J. said in *Mid-City Skin Cancer & Laser Centre v Zahedi-Anarak* [2006] NSWSC 844 at [273], It is not the case that such allowances are "ordinarily made".

NOTE 35. ADD: See, e.g., *Say-Dee Pty Ltd v Farah Constructions Pty Ltd* [2005] NSWCA 309 at [252], where an allowance was given, despite "a not insignificant degree of surreptitious conduct and bad faith" on the part of the fiduciary, but the court made clear that "any such allowance should not be liberal". Similarly, in *Murad v Al-Saraj* [2005] EWCA Civ 959 an allowance was made (see at [88]) despite the deceitful conduct of the fiduciary.

NOTE 36. ADD: This paragraph was quoted in *Imageview Management Ltd v Jack* [2009] EWCA Civ 63 at [56].

ADD AT END OF PARAGRAPH: This is not to say that the fiduciary's liability to account is based on the concept of unjust enrichment; rather, the remedy of an account is a conventional remedy for a breach of fiduciary duty but one which must not be allowed to become a vehicle for the unjust enrichment of the claimant: *Warman International Ltd v Dwyer* (1995) 182 CLR 544 at 561; *Murad v Al-Saraj* [2005] EWCA Civ 959 at [64].

ADD AT END OF PARAGRAPH: Although an account of profits is an equitable remedy, and so subject to the court's discretion, the fiduciary's principal is entitled to an account of profits made in breach of fiduciary duty virtually as of right: *Warman International Ltd. v Dwyer* (1995) 182 C.L.R. 544, 560. McLachlin C.J. has recently suggested, obiter, that this perhaps ought not to be the case: *Strother v 3464920 Canada Inc* [2007] SCC 24 at [152]–[158]. Her analysis ignores relevant authority, relies on irrelevant material, and is entirely misguided. She ignores the High Court of Australia's decision in *Warman v Dwyer*, which dealt with the very point at issue. She quotes from, and relies on, David Hayton's suggestions as to whether a *proprietary* remedy ought to be available in such circumstances (as opposed to a merely *personal* remedy), which is irrelevant to the question whether the orthodox *profit-stripping* remedy of an account should be unavailable where no *loss* has been caused. Her suggestion is akin to the defendant's argument in *Murad v Al-Saraj* [2005] EWCA Civ 959 that liability to account for profits made in breach of fiduciary duty ought to be limited to the loss that the claimant has suffered, which was rightly rejected by the English Court of Appeal (see the discussion in [2006] C.L.J. 278). English law has rejected that argument for hundreds of years, and it ought to continue to do so, in spite of McLachlin C.J.'s analysis.

3. Forfeiture of fees

NOTE 37. ADD: *Oceanic Life Ltd v HIH Casualty & General Insurance Ltd* [1999] NSWSC 292 at [42].   **7–132**

NOTE 40. ADD: *Stevens v Premium Real Estate Ltd* [2009] NZSC 15 at [89].   **7–133**

NOTE 41. ADD: *Imageview Management Ltd v Jack* [2009] EWCA Civ 63 at [44] & [46].

NOTE 42. ADD: *Imageview Management Ltd v Jack* [2009] EWCA Civ 63 at [47]–[50].

4. Equitable compensation for loss

NOTE 44. ADD: *Breen v Williams* (1996) 186 C.L.R. 71 at pp.113 & 135–136;   **7–135**
Rama v Millar [1996] 1 N.Z.L.R. 257 (PC); *Aequitas v AEFC* [2001] NSWSC 14, (2001) 19 A.C.L.C. 1,006 at [428] & [442]; *Re MDA Investment Management Ltd* [2003] EWHC 227 (Ch) at [70]; *Cassis v Kalfus (No 2)* [2004] NSWCA 315 at [99]; *Wilson v Hurstanger Ltd* [2007] EWCA Civ 299 at [34]–[35] & [49]; *Schipp v Cameron* [1998] NSWSC 997 at [741]; *PNC Telecom plc v Thomas (No 2)* [2007] EWHC 2157 (Ch) at [89], [2008] 2 B.C.L.C. 95.

7–138   NOTE 58. ADD: *Halton International Inc (Holding) SARL v Guernroy Ltd* [2005] EWHC 1968 (Ch) at [155]; *Blythe v Northwood* [2005] NSWCA 221 at [78]; *Stevens v Premium Real Estate Ltd* [2009] NZSC 15.

NOTE 59. ADD: *Murad v Al-Saraj* [2005] EWCA Civ 959 at [110] & [120]; *Aequitas v AEFC* [2001] NSWSC 14, (2001) 19 A.C.L.C. 1,006 at [443]–[448]; *Edmonds v Donovan* [2005] V.S.C.A. 27 at [78]. In *Take v BSM Marketing* [2006] EWHC 1085 (Q.B.), an agent was found to have acted in breach of fiduciary duty by competing with his principal, but was only liable to pay compensation for losses which would not have been suffered but for his breaches of duty: at [189] & [206].

NOTE 60. ADD: *Gwembe Valley Development Co Ltd v Koshy* [2003] EWCA Civ 1478; [2004] 1 BCLC 131 at [147] and [159].

NOTE 61. ADD: The defendant director in *Gwembe Valley Development Co Ltd v Koshy* [2003] EWCA Civ 1478; [2004] 1 B.C.L.C. 131 was found to have acted dishonestly in not disclosing his interest in a transaction and was nonetheless held not liable to pay equitable compensation on the basis that his breach had not been proven to have caused loss to his company: see [135] and [159].

NOTE 62. DELETE ENTIRE NOTE AND REPLACE WITH FOLLOWING: *Swindle v Harrison*, above, at 718, 726 & 733. Thus, the primary onus is on the principal (or beneficiary) to show that "but for the breach, the beneficiary would not have acted in the way which has caused his loss": *Nationwide Building Society v Balmer Radmore (Introductory Sections)* [1999] Lloyd's Rep. P.N. 241 at 278. If this onus is met, the court may draw inferences (but cannot merely speculate) as to what would have happened if the fiduciary had performed his duty properly, and in the absence of evidence to justify such inferences the beneficiary is entitled to be placed in the position he was in before the breach occurred, unless the fiduciary (on whom the onus will lie) is able to show what the principal (or beneficiary) would have done if there had been no breach of fiduciary duty: *Balmer Radmore*, above at 278–279. This approach, which places the onus on the fiduciary after the beneficiary has met an initial burden of proof is slightly different from the approach in Canada and New Zealand where, adapting the Privy Council's comment in *Brickenden v London Loan & Savings Co* [1934] 3 D.L.R. 465 at 469, it has been held that the fiduciary bears the burden of proving that the principal would have acted in the same way if it wishes to avoid an award of compensation; and mere speculation will not suffice to convince the court of this, but inferences can be drawn from the evidence where they are clear: *Commerce Capital Trust Co v Berk* (1989) 68 O.R. (2d.) 257 at 261; *Hodgkinson v Simms* (1994) 117 D.L.R. (4th.) 161 at 200; *Everist v McEvedy* [1996] 3 N.Z.L.R. 348 at 355; *Gilbert v Shanahan* [1998] 3 N.Z.L.R. 528 at 535; *Bank of New Zealand v New Zealand Guardian Trust Co Ltd* [1999] 1 N.Z.L.R. 664 at 687; *Taylor v Schofield Peterson* [1999] 3 N.Z.L.R. 434 at 445–446; *Maruha Corp v Amaltal Corp Ltd* [2007] NZSC 40 at [30]. However, the difference in approach is unlikely to matter in terms of the practical outcome of most cases: even in *Swindle v Harrison*, where the onus of proof was on Mrs Harrison, her claim *failed* not because she had failed to show that she would have acted differently, but because it was *clear* from the evidence that she would not have acted differently.

ADD AT END OF PARAGRAPH: If causation is made out so that a compensation award is available, the fiduciary does not avoid responsibility to compensate for the full amount of that loss by having diverted a profitable opportunity to a partnership (or other vehicle) which is only partly owned by the fiduciary: *Re MDA Investment Management Ltd* [2004] EWHC 42 (Ch) at [4].

ADD NEW PARAGRAPH: (e) *Interest.* Interest may be awarded on an **7–140A** equitable compensation order, and may be awarded on a compound basis: *Alenco (Holdings) Ltd v Bates* [2005] EWHC 1540 (Ch) at [50]; *Wallersteiner v Moir (No 2)* [1975] Q.B. 373 at 388 & 397–398. Compound interest is available in respect of any monetary award made consequent upon a breach of fiduciary duty: *Primlake Ltd (in liq) v Matthews Associates* [2006] EWHC 1227 (Ch) at [343].

NOTE 66. ADD: *De Beer v Kanaar & Co* [2002] EWHC 688 (Ch) at [92] **7–140** (where the point is asserted, in the context of a trust claim, without discussion).

NOTE 68. ADD: The New Zealand Supreme Court appears recently to have reversed this, but the status of its comment remains unclear as it is made in a mere footnote and without any reference to, let alone analysis of, *Day v Mead*: see *Maruha Corp v Amaltal International Ltd* [2007] NZSC 40 at [23(fn.17)].

NOTE 72. ADD: *Sphere Drake Insurance Ltd v Euro International Underwriting Ltd* [2003] EWHC 1636 (Comm) at [96]–[97], [2003] Lloyd's Rep IR 525.

5. Proprietary remedies

ADD NEW NOTE AT END OF LAST SENTENCE: NOTE 77A: *In Plus Group Ltd v Pyke* **7–141** [2002] EWCA Civ 370 at [71], [2002] 2 BCLC 201.

NOTE 82. ADD: See also *Zobory v Federal Commissioner of Taxation* (1995) **7–143** 129 A.L.R. 484, where a similar conclusion was reached where an employee stole money from his employer and invested it profitably.

NOTE 84. ADD: See also *Ultraframe (UK) Ltd v Fielding* [2005] EWHC 1638 (Ch) at [1490]; *Primlake Ltd (in liq) v Matthews Associates* [2006] EWHC 1227 (Ch) at [334]; *Pakistan v Zardari* [2006] EWHC 2411 (Comm) at [164]; *Sinclair Investment Holdings SA v Versailles Trade Finance Ltd* [2007] EWHC 915 (Ch) at [105]. *Reid* has also been followed in Australia: *Mainland Holdings Ltd v Szady* [2002] NSWSC 699.

ADD AT END OF PARAGRAPH: Similarly, in *Bhullar v Bhullar* [2003] EWCA Civ 424, [2003] 2 B.C.L.C. 241 the Court of Appeal confirmed that directors held property on constructive trust for their company after they acquired it for themselves in circumstances involving a conflict between the directors' duty to the company and their personal interest in the property.

7–144   ADD AT BEGINNING OF NOTE 85: *Ultraframe (UK) Ltd v Fielding* [2005] EWHC 1638 (Ch) at [1519].

7. Limitation periods

7–148   NOTE 96. ADD: See, *e.g.*, *Johns v Johns* [2004] NZCA 42 at [68], [2005] W.T.L.R. 529. See generally Mather, "Fiduciaries and the law of limitation" [2008] J.B.L. 344. And see Stafford & Ritchie, *Fiduciary Duties: Directors and Employees* (2008) ch 10.

7–149   ADD AT END OF PARAGRAPH: Nor does the six-year limitation period apply where the fiduciary has deliberately concealed from his principal any fact relevant to the principal's cause of action, such as where a fiduciary consciously decided not to disclose his interest in a transaction with his principal and realised that the fact suppressed related to his original wrongdoing: Limitation Act 1980, s.32(1)(b); *Newgate Stud Co v Penfold* [2004] EWHC 2993 (Ch) at [252]–[256].

NOTE 99. ADD: *Bank of Credit & Commerce International SA (in liq) v Saadi* [2005] EWHC 2256 (QB) at [30]–[31].

7–150   NOTE 5. ADD: see also *Halton International Inc (Holding) SARL v Guernroy Ltd* [2005] EWHC 1968 (Ch) at [164]; *Halton International Inc v Guernroy Ltd* [2006] EWCA Civ 801 at [10]–[23].

NOTE 6. ADD: see also *Halton International Inc v Guernroy Ltd* [2006] EWCA Civ 801 at [18].

NOTE 7. ADD: although see now the explanation given in *Halton International Inc v Guernroy Ltd* [2006] EWCA Civ 801 at [22] fn.1, where *Gwembe* is explained as a case based on fraudulent concealment rather than mere fraud.

7–151   NOTE 9. ADD: *Cattley v Pollard* [2006] EWHC 3130 (Ch), [2007] 2 All E.R. 1086 at [149].

END SENTENCE AFTER NOTE 9 AND ADD THE FOLLOWING NEW SENTENCE: The defence of laches can potentially apply even if the Limitation Act 1980 makes it clear that no statutory period of limitation applies: *Re Loftus (deceased)* [2006] EWCA Civ 1124, [2007] 1 W.L.R. 591 at [40]–[41], disapproving apparently contrary observations in *Gwembe Valley Development Co Ltd v Koshy* [2003] EWCA Civ 1478 at [140]; see also *Cattley v Pollard* [2006] EWHC 3130 (Ch), [2007] 2 All E.R. 1086 at [151]; *Patel v Shah* [2005] EWCA Civ 157 at [22].

7–152A   ADD NEW PARAGRAPH: **8. Removal** A fiduciary who acts in a situation involving actual or potential conflict between duties owed to more than one client, may be prevented, by way of injunction, from continuing to act: *Marks & Spencer plc v Freshfields Bruckhaus Deringer* [2004] EWHC 1337 (Ch); [2004] 1 W.L.R. 2331. The conflict must be more than a mere theoretical possibility; there must be a reasonable apprehension of a potential conflict before an injunction will issue: *Marks & Spencer plc v Freshfields Bruckhaus Deringer* [2004] EWHC 1337 (Ch); [2004] 1 W.L.R. 2331 at [15]; *Re Baron Investments (Holdings) Ltd (in liq)* [2000] 1 B.C.L.C. 272 at 282–284. The availability of such an injunction is not limited to cases where the conflict arises in respect of a single matter involving the two (or more) clients to whom inconsistent duties are owed, but where this is not the case an injunction is not available unless there is a reasonable relationship between the two matters: *Marks & Spencer plc v Freshfields Bruckhaus Deringer* [2004] EWHC 1337 (Ch); [2004] 1 W.L.R. 2331 at [16]. Similarly, directors of companies who have acted in breach of the fiduciary duties which they owe to their company can be removed: see, *e.g.*, *Secretary of State for Trade and Industry v Paulin* [2005] EWHC 888 (ChD).

7. RELATIONSHIP TO OTHER EQUITABLE DOCTRINES OF PROTECTION

2. Confidence

NOTE 29. ADD: *Ratiu v Conway* [2005] EWCA Civ 1302 at [56]; *R v Neil* [2002] S.C.C. 70, [2002] 3 S.C.R. 631 at [17]; *Paper Reclaim Ltd v Aotearoa International Ltd* [2007] NZSC 26 at [32].   **7–159**

NOTE 32. ADD: *Oceanic Life Ltd v HIH Casualty & General Insurance Ltd* [1999] NSWSC 292 at [44] & [55].   **7–160**

Chapter 8

FRAUD AND UNDUE INFLUENCE

3. Undue Influence

1. The Doctrine

NOTE 66. ADD. In *Daniel v Drew* [2005] EWCA Civ 507, [2005] W.T.L.R.   **8–11**
807 the Court set aside a deed of retirement of a trustee which was
procured by undue influence.

NOTE 67. ADD: For undue influence in relation to wills see now the in
depth analysis in Ridge "Equitable Undue Influence and Wills" [2004]
120 L.Q.R. 617. Ridge's thesis is that there is no principled reason for the
continued distinction between the equitable doctrine of undue influence
and the probate doctrine of undue influence. ADD: See also *Cattermole v
Prisk* [2006] 1 F.L.R. 697 (which involved both testamentary and inter
vivos gifts) at [13] and *Re Wilkes* [2006] W.T.L.R. 1097

NOTE 72. ADD: In *Daniel v Drew* [2005] EWCA Civ 507, [2005] W.T.L.R.   **8–12**
807 at [36] Ward L.J. offered the following description of the dividing
line: "In all cases of undue influence the critical question is whether or
not the persuasion or the advice, in other words the influence, has
invaded the free volition of the donor to accept or reject the persuasion
or advice or withstand the influence. The donor may be led but she
must not be driven and her will must be the offspring of her own
volition, not a record of someone else's. There is no undue influence
unless the donor if she were free and informed could say "This is not
my wish but I must do it".'

NOTE 79. ADD: For a recent example of case in which the receipt of legal
advice was insufficient to rebut the presumption see *Wright v Hodgkinson* [2005] W.T.L.R. 435 (no neutral citation).

NOTE 80. ADD: See also *Michael v Cansick* [2004] EWHC 1684 (Ch) in
which a grandfather executed a lifetime transfer to his granddaughter
after consulting his son-in-law (who was or had been a solicitor). When
other members of the family challenged the transfer it was upheld. The
judge also noted that to give rise to the presumption of undue influence
it was not necessary to show influence was exerted in relation to the
questioned transaction.

NOTE 81. ADD: See *Turkey v Awadh* [2005] EWCA Civ 382, [2006]
W.T.L.R. 553 where C did receive advice from a solicitor (albeit not

independent and through an interpreter) and where the issue was whether the failure of the parties to determine whether the price paid for a property was a fair one called for explanation and therefore gave rise to the presumption of undue influence. The judge found that the transaction, although unusual, could be explained without resort to the presumption of undue influence and that the burden did not shift to D. The C.A. upheld this conclusion.

8–13   NOTE 87. ADD: For another example of what amounts to actual undue influence see *Daniel v Drew* [2005] EWCA Civ 507, [2005] W.T.L.R. 807 at [45] to [47].

8–16   NOTE 98: For an example of a presumed undue influence case where all of the parties gave evidence see *Turkey v Awadh* [2005] EWCA Civ 382, [2005] W.T.L.R. 553. In that case the CA upheld the trial judge's decision that the claim failed because the transaction could be properly explained. He held, however, that if the presumption arose it could not be rebutted.

NOTE 99. ADD: For an attempt to reconcile *Etridge and Hammond v Osborn see Randall v Randall* [2005] W.T.L.R. 119 (no neutral citation) at [36] to [45].

NOTE 1. ADD: For continued support of the public policy approach see *Cattermole v Prisk* [2006] W.T.L.R. 1097.

8–19   NOTE 22. ADD: See also *Macklin v Dowsett* [2004] EWCA Civ 904 (vendor and purchaser).

8–28   AMEND TEXT TO NOTE 63 SO AS TO READ AS FOLLOWS: They explained that manifest disadvantage means "an advantage taken of the person subjected to the influence which, failing proof to the contrary, was explicable *only* on the basis that undue influence had been exercised to procure it."

NOTE 72. ADD: For other examples of imbalance of benefits see *Humphreys v Humphreys* [2004] EWHC 2201 (Ch) (mother and son acquiring mother's council house at a discount and mother entering into a deed of trust under which son's consent required for sale and son entitled to proceeds of sale in return for which son paid the mortgage); and *Macklin v Dowsett* [2004] EWCA Civ 904 (life tenant of property granted option to purchase property for £5,000 if a bungalow not built on it within 3 years).

8–31   NOTE 95. ADD: For anothjer recent example of a case in which the receipt of legal advice was insufficient to rebut the presumption see *Wright v Hodgkinson* [2005] W.T.L.R. 435 (no neutral citation). In that case the Court also found that the advice was insufficient to bring home to C the implications of the transaction.

8–39A   ADD AT END OF PARAGRAPH NEW PARAGRAPH (F) *Substitute Mortgages*
In *Yorkshire Bank plc v Tinsley* [NOTE 22A] the Court has recently had to consider the validity of a security which was substituted for a security

which was liable to be set aside for undue influence. The Court of Appeal held that a mortgage which was substituted for a voidable mortgage would itself be voidable even though there was no operative undue influence when it was taken. The principle only applies, however, where the mortgage is taken by the same mortgagee and is inseparably connected with the earlier security. Further, although the undue influence may no longer be operative, the substitute mortgage will be upheld if it has been cured (e.g. by the affirmation of the mortgagor).

NOTE 22A. [2004] EWCA Civ 816. See also Gravells "Undue Influence and Substitute Mortgages" [2005] 64 C.L.J 42.

NOTE 24. ADD: See also *Humphreys v Humphreys* [2004] EWHC 2201 **8–40** (Ch) at [103] (4 years delay not sufficient to bar claim for undue influence).

NOTE 43. ADD: Followed in *Cattermole v Prisk* [2006] W.T.L.R. 1097.   **8–44**

CHAPTER 10

ESTOPPEL

1. SOURCES OF THE MODERN LAW OF ESTOPPEL

2. Estoppel in equity

ADD TEXT: In *Yeoman's Row Management Ltd v Cobbe* [2008] UKHL 55, **10–4**
[2008] 1 W.L.R. 1752 the House of Lords has now confirmed that
unconscionable conduct by itself is insufficient to give rise to a valid
claim for proprietary estoppel and that in order to give rise to an
estoppel the claim must be capable of being analysed in the traditional
manner. In that case there was an informal agreement (which both
parties appreciated was not legally binding) between a property owner
and a property developer that the developer would apply for planning
permission for the property, that if planning permission was granted the
owner would sell the property to the developer and the developer
would pay 50% of the profits from the development to the owner above
a certain figure. When planning permission was obtained, the owner
refused to be bound by the agreement. At first instance Etherton J
([2005] EWHC 266 (Ch)) held that this gave rise to a proprietary
estoppel which entitled the developer to recover 50% of the increase in
value of the property due to the grant of planning permission and the
Court of Appeal dismissed the appeal: see [2006] EWCA Civ 1139,
[2006] 1 W.L.R. 2964. The House of Lords allowed the owner's appeal
and held that the agreement did not give rise to a proprietary estoppel
and that the developer's remedy was limited to a quantum meruit. The
relationship between proprietary estoppel and constructive trust (and, in
particular, the need for a promise that the claimant will acquire a
specific interest in property) has been considered in a number of recent
cases. In *Cobbe*, the House of Lords also held that the agreement
between the parties did not give rise to a constructive trust.

ADD FOOTNOTE 25A [after *"quantum meruit"* above]:

At [14] Lord Scott (with whom Lord Hoffmann, Lord Brown and Lord
Mance agreed) stated:

"Both the learned judge and the Court of Appeal regarded the relief
granted as justified on the basis of proprietary estoppel. I respectfully
disagree. The remedy to which, on the facts as found by the judge,
Mr Cobbe is entitled can, in my opinion, be described neither as

based on an estoppel nor as proprietary in character. There are several important authorities to which I want to refer but I want first to consider as a matter of principle the nature of a proprietary estoppel. An "estoppel" bars the object of it from asserting some fact or facts, or, sometimes, something that is a mixture of fact and law, that stands in the way of some right claimed by the person entitled to the benefit of the estoppel. The estoppel becomes a "proprietary" estoppel - a sub-species of a "promissory" estoppel - if the right claimed is a proprietary right, usually a right to or over land but, in principle, equally available in relation to chattels or choses in action."

At [16] he also stated: "My Lords, unconscionability of conduct may well lead to a remedy but, in my opinion, proprietary estoppel cannot be the route to it unless the ingredients for a proprietary estoppel are present. These ingredients should include, in principle, a proprietary claim made by a Claimant and an answer to that claim based on some fact, or some point of mixed fact and law, that the person against whom the claim is made can be estopped from asserting. To treat a "proprietary estoppel equity" as requiring neither a proprietary claim by the Claimant nor an estoppel against the Defendant but simply unconscionable behaviour is, in my respectful opinion, a recipe for confusion."

Lord Walker (who delivered a concurring judgment) described the use of the word "unconscionable" at [92] in the following terms:

"Here it is being used (as in my opinion it should always be used) as an objective value judgment on behaviour (regardless of the state of mind of the individual in question). As such it does in my opinion play a very important part in the doctrine of equitable estoppel, in unifying and confirming, as it were, the other elements. If the other elements appear to be present but the result does not shock the conscience of the court, the analysis needs to be looked at again. In this case Mrs Lisle-Mainwaring's conduct was unattractive. She chose to stand on her rights rather than respecting her non-binding assurances, while Mr Cobbe continued to spend time and effort, between Christmas 2003 and March 2004, in obtaining planning permission. But Mr Cobbe knew that she was bound in honour only, and so in the eyes of equity her conduct, although unattractive, was not unconscionable."

ADD FOOTNOTE 25B: See *Cobbe* (above) at [30] to [37] (where Lord Scott held that an agreement binding in honour only could not give rise to a constructive trust). See also *Oxley v Hiscock* [2004] EWCA Civ 546, [2004] 2 F.L.R. 669, *Van Laethem v Brooker* [2005] EWHC 1478 (Ch), [2006] 2 F.L.R. 495 (Lawrence Collins J) at [61] to [82], *Turner v Jacob* [2006] EWHC 1317 (Ch), [2008] W.T.L.R. 307 and *James v Thomas* [2007] EWCA Civ 1212, [2008] 1 FLR 1598. In the latter case Chadwick LJ examined the assurances made by the defendant and held that they were insufficiently specific to give rise to a proprietary estoppel: see [33] to [38]. *James v Thomas* was applied in *Morris v Morris* [2008] EWCA Civ 257 with the same result.

ADD TO FOOTNOTE 32: In *Yeoman's Row Management Ltd v Cobbe* [2008]   **10–5**
UKHL 55 Lord Scott described proprietary estoppel as "a sub-species of 'promissory estoppel'" which becomes a "proprietary estoppel" if the right claimed is a property right or over land or chattels.

NOTE 37. ADD: For a good example of the difference between a shared   **10–6**
understanding and a convention which regulates the parties dealings see *Bridgestart Properties Ltd v London Underground Ltd* [2004] EWCA Civ 793 in which both parties were unaware that a limitation period had expired but continued to negotiate the terms of statutory compensation. It was held that there was no estoppel by convention because there was no convention that E would not take any limitation defence. Nor was there any unequivocal representation which would give rise to a promissory estoppel.

NOTE 71. ADD: For an example of a case in which the Court was not   **10–9**
prepared to imply a promise or assurance from silence see *Northstar Land Ltd v Brooks* [2006] EWCA Civ 756, [2006] 2 E.G.L.R. 67 where a solicitor failed to respond to a request for an extension of time to complete. The conclusion of the Court was stated by Ward L.J. at [28]:

> "In my judgment, just as the statement, "I will take instructions" is equivocal, so too was the silence that followed. Viewed objectively, no reasonably competent solicitor having conduct of an important completion like this would have understood from the silence of the other side that they were agreeing to postpone completion. It was, after all, Mr Drew who began chasing Faegre Benson shortly after noon by his email which clearly indicated his clients' readiness to complete. His messages after three o'clock reaffirmed that the message was urgent and related to completion of the option. It should have set alarm bells ringing but Miss Albery appears to have been deaf to them. There was certainly, in my judgment, no justification whatever for her believing that the vendors' manifest readiness to complete had been replaced by a willingness to postpone that completion for a week."

NOTE 24. ADD: In *Riverside Housing Ltd v White* [2005] EWCA Civ 1385,   **10–14**
[2006] 14 E.G. 176, [2006] H.L.R. 282 (reversed on different grounds by the House of Lords at [2007] UKHL 20, [2007] 4 All E.R. 97) the Court of Appeal held that an estoppel by convention could not be used to sustain a claim for rent arrears by a landlord against a tenant. In that case the landlord had served a unilateral notice increasing the rent (which it was entitled to do) but the notice was expressed to take effect at a date which was later than that provided for in the tenancy agreement. The Court of Appeal held that the notice was ineffective as a matter of

contract and although all of the ingredients of an estoppel by convention were made out, the claim failed on the basis that the estoppel could not be used a sword rather than a shield: see [59] to [67]. In both *Baird* and *Riverside* the Court of Appeal confirmed that an estoppel of this kind could only be used as a sword if the House of Lords so decides. Permission to appeal to the House of Lords has now been given.

NOTE 26. ADD: For an example of a case in which promissory estoppel was raised as a defence to a claim for possession see *Babar v Anis* [2005] EWHC 1384 (Ch) (Richard Arnold QC). It would be absurd if the outcome depended on whether D had brought a claim for a declaration or whether she based her claim on promissory estoppel rather than proprietary estoppel.

3. PROPRIETARY ESTOPPEL

1. The equity

10–16 NOTE 44: ADD: Cited with approval by Lord Scott in *Yeoman's Row Management Ltd v Cobbe* [2008] UKHL 55, [2008] 1 W.L.R. 1752 at [18] and Lord Walker at [56] to [59]. Note that Lord Scott laid emphasis on the importance of the words "a certain interest in land".

NOTE 46: ADD: See now the analysis of Lords Walker in *Yeoman's Row Management Ltd v Cobbe* [2008] UKHL 55, [2008] 1 W.L.R. 1752 (above) at [49] to [65] dividing the cases into "imperfect gift" cases such as *Dilwyn v Llewellyn* or "unilateral mistake" cases to which the *Wilmott v Barber* probanda would apply. He stated at [65] that ". . . hopes by themselves are not enough. . . ".

NOTE 50. ADD: For a recent example of a proprietary estoppel arising in relation to the benefit of an insurance policy see *Strover v Strover* [2005] EWHC 860 (Ch). See also para.10–22, note 22.

NOTE 52. ADD: For an example of an intellectual property case see *Fisher v Brooker* [2009] UKHL 41, [2009] 1 W.L.R. 1764. The claim (which was based on acquiescence over a 40 year period) failed on the facts.

10–17 NOTE 73. ADD: In *Thorner v Major* [2008] EWCA Civ 732 a claim that the deceased's estate was estopped from denying that his farm should pass to another family member failed on the ground that the promise or assurance by the deceased was not sufficiently clear and unequivocal or intended to be relied on: see [72] to [74]. The assurance was, however, implicit and based on conduct.

NOTE 72. The decision of the Court of Appeal has now been reversed by the House of Lords: *Thorner v Major* [2009] UKHL [2009] 1 WLR 776. The decision of the House of Lords was also followed by Lewison J in *Thompson v Foy* [2009] EWHC 1076 (Ch).

NOTE 74. ADD: "In *Sutcliffe v Lloyd* [2007] EWCA Civ 153, [2007] 22 EG 162 the Court of Appeal held that it is not necessary to the creation of a proprietary estoppel that the promisor should have made it clear that its promise was irrevocable or enforceable in law. They also held (following *Yeoman's Row Management Ltd v Cobbe* [2006] EWCA Civ 1139, [2006] 1 W.L.R. 2964) that the crucial matter was that the appellants had given assurances to the respondent and allowed him to act to his detriment upon them such as to make clear that those assurances would not in fact be revoked. Both the decision and the proposition in the text must now be read in the light of the decision of the House of Lords in *Cobbe* at [2008] UKHL 55, [2008] 1 W.L.R. 1752 where the decision of the Court of Appeal was reversed and the claim of proprietary estoppel failed. In that case there was an informal agreement between the parties in a commercial context and the Court reached a similar conclusion to that of the Privy Counsel in *Att-Gen of Hong Kong v Humphreys Estate* [1987] A.C. 114 (referred to in note 75). At [27] Lord Scott stated:

"My Lords, I can easily accept that a subject-to-contract reservation made in the course of negotiations for a contract relating to the acquisition of an interest in land could be withdrawn, whether expressly or by inference from conduct. But debate about subject-to-contract reservations has only a peripheral relevance in the present case, for such a reservation is pointless in the context of oral negotiations relating to the acquisition of an interest in land. It would be an unusually unsophisticated negotiator who was not well aware that oral agreements relating to such an acquisition are by statute unenforceable and that no express reservation to make them so is needed. Mr Cobbe was an experienced property developer and Mrs Lisle-Mainwaring gives every impression of knowing her way around the negotiating table. Mr Cobbe did not spend his money and time on the planning application in the mistaken belief that the agreement was legally enforceable. He spent his money and time well aware that it was not. Mrs Lisle-Mainwaring did not encourage in him a belief that the second agreement was enforceable. She encouraged in him a belief that she would abide by it although it was not. Mr Cobbe's belief, or expectation, was always speculative. He knew she was not legally bound. He regarded her as bound "in honour" but that is an acknowledgement that she was not legally bound."

Lord Walker examined the difference between domestic cases like *Gillett v Holt* and commercial negotiations at [66] to [81]. He concluded (at [81]) that: "In my opinion none of these cases casts any doubt on the general principle laid down by this House in *Ramsden v Dyson*, that conscious reliance on honour alone will not give rise to an estoppel. Nor do they cast doubt on the general principle that the court should be very slow to introduce uncertainty into commercial transactions by over-ready use of equitable concepts such as fiduciary obligations and equitable estoppel. That applies to commercial negotiations whether or not they are expressly stated to be subject to contract."

10–18

NOTE 91. ADD: In *Uglow v Uglow* [2004] EWCA Civ 987 the Court of Appeal distinguished *Gillett v Holt* and held that an assurance to leave property in a willdid not become irrevocable because it was based on the premise that T and C would remain in partnership. It was also held that C's equity had in substance been satisfied by the grant of an agricultural tenancy. This case adds to the confusion in that it remains difficult to identify or distill the features which will make an assurance irrevocable.

10–19 NOTE 2. ADD: See also the discussion of *Holiday Inns Inc v Broadhead in Yeoman's Row Management Ltd v Cobbe* [2008] UKHL 55, [2008] 1 W.L.R. 1752 at [24] (Lord Scott) and [76] to [78] (Lord Walker) where both considered that it is better treated as an example of the application of the *Pallant v Morgan* equity.

NOTE 8. ADD: But see now *Chadwick v Abbotswood Properties Ltd* [2004] EWHC 1058 (Ch) at [69] to [70] in which Lewison J held that Ds' expenditure on their own land gave rise to an estoppel in the context of a boundary agreement.

NOTE 9. ADD: In *Murphy v Burrows* [2004] EWHC 1900 (Ch) Richard Sheldon QC held that the detriment incurred by C (additional work worth £7,825 in cash terms) was insufficiently substantial to make it inequitable for T to withdraw his assurances and change his will. He also held that if this was wrong a monetary remedy would have been suitable.

10–20 NOTE 18. ADD: For a further example, see *Scottish & Newcastle plc v Lancashire Mortgage Corporation Ltd* [2007] EWCA Civ 684, [2007] N.P.C. 84 where the Court of Appeal held that one mortgagee was estopped from asserting that on the sale of a property it was entitled to be paid ahead of payment to the other: see Mummery L.J.'s conclusion at [59]. The Court of Appeal rejected a submission that the mortgagee raising the estoppel could not rely on it because the transaction contravened section 2(1) of the Law of Property (Miscellaneous Provisions) Act 1989: see [50] to [58]. This and the other cases referred to in note 18 must now be read in the light of *Cobbe v Yeomans Row Management Ltd* [2008] UKHL 55. In that case Etherton J. held that an informal agreement that C would obtain an interest in a development property if he obtained planning permission was held binding as a proprietary estoppel and was not defeated by the fact that the parties did not intend a formal agreement to come into existence until after planning permission was granted. The decision of Etherton J. was upheld by the Court of Appeal but has now been overruled by the House of Lords at [2008] UKHL 55. On the application of the statute Lord Scott stated this at [29] (and Lord Walker agreed with his conclusion at [93]):

"There is one further point regarding proprietary estoppel to which I should refer. Section 2 of the 1989 Act declares to be void any agreement for the acquisition of an interest in land that does not comply with the requisite formalities prescribed by the section. Sub-section (5) expressly makes an exception for resulting, implied or constructive trusts. These may validly come into existence without compliance with the prescribed formalities. Proprietary estoppel does not have the benefit of this exception. The question arises, therefore, whether a complete agreement for the acquisition of an interest in land that does not comply with the s 2 prescribed formalities, but would be specifically enforceable if it did, can become enforceable via the route of proprietary estoppel. It is not necessary in the present case to answer this question, for the second agreement was not a complete agreement and, for that reason, would not have been specifically enforceable so long as it remained incomplete. My present view, however, is that proprietary estoppel cannot be prayed in aid in order to render enforceable an agreement that statute has declared to be void. The proposition that an owner of land can be estopped from asserting that an agreement is void for want of compliance with the requirements of s 2 is, in my opinion, unacceptable. The assertion is no more than the statute provides. Equity can surely not contradict the statute. As I have said, however, statute provides an express exception for constructive trusts. So to Mr Cobbe's constructive trust claim I must now turn."

The constructive trust claim also failed: see [30] to [37] The defendant already owned the property and the facts of the case (set out in para.10–04 above) did not give rise to a constructive trust. Lord Scott stated this (at [37]):

"The unconscionable behaviour of Mrs Lisle-Mainwaring is, in my opinion, not enough in the circumstances of this case to justify Mr Cobbe's claim to have acquired, or to be awarded by the court, a beneficial interest in the property. The salient features of the case that preclude that claim are, to my mind, that the Appellant owned the property before Mr Cobbe came upon the scene, that the second agreement produced by the discussions between him and Mrs Lisle-Mainwaring was known to both to be legally unenforceable, that an unenforceable promise to perform a legally unenforceable agreement - which is what an agreement "binding in honour" comes to - can give no greater advantage than the unenforceable agreement, that Mr Cobbe's expectation of an enforceable contract, on the basis of which he applied for and obtained the grant of planning permission, was inherently speculative and contingent on Mrs Lisle-Mainwaring's decisions regarding the incomplete agreement and that Mr Cobbe never expected to acquire an interest in the property otherwise than under a legally enforceable contract. In these circumstances the imposition of the constructive trust on the property and the *pro tanto* divesting of the Appellant's ownership of it seems to me more in the nature of an indignant reaction to Mrs Lisle-Mainwaring's unconscionable behaviour than a principled answer to Mr Cobbe's claim for relief."

It is suggested that *Yaxley v Gotts* and *Scottish & Newcastle plc v Lancashire Mortgage Corporation Ltd* (above) and other cases amy be distinguished from *Cobbe* because the facts were sufficient to give rise to a genuine constructive trust. For instance in *Scottish & Newcastle* the Court of Appeal did not reverse the order of priorities but imposed a constructive trust over the proceeds of sale: see [56] to [58]. See also *Kinane v Mackie-Conteh* [2005] EWCA Civ 45 [2005] 2 P. & C.R. DG3. This case (and *Cobbe* at first instance) are discussed in [2005] 69 Conv 247.

10–21 NOTE 25. ADD: For consideration of the position since 1999 (and, in particular, the CA's decision in *Jennings v Rice*) see Gardner *The Remedial Discretion in Proprietary Estoppel—Again* (2006) 122 L.Q.R. 492.

10–22 NOTE 38. ADD: In *Strover v Strover* [2005] EWHC 860 (Ch) the Court reduced the value of C's interest in an insurance policy to take account of the fact that Es might not have assigned the benefit to him if he had lived.

NOTE 40. ADD: See also *Clark v Clark* [2006] EWHC 275 (Ch), [2006] W.T.L.R. 823 at [28] to [37] where Blackburne J helpfully distilled from *Jennings v Rice* the proposition that the Court's approach "must to some extent turn on the clarity with which the Claimant's expectation and the element of detriment to him have been defined". For further analysis and criticism of the exercise of the discretion post *Jennings v Rice* see Gardner *The Remedial Discretion in Proprietary Estoppel—Again* (2006) 122 L.Q.R. 492.

10–23 NOTE 44. ADD: For an example of a case in which relief was refused because of A's own conduct in refusing to honour the terms of the agreement see *Horton v Brandish* (*Hart J.*, unreported 29 July 2005) [no neutral citation]. See, in particular, [38] and [39]: "The son simply thought he could get away with not honouring the agreement. This was a catastrophic misjudgement on his part."

NOTE 45. ADD: In *McGuane v Welch* [2008] EWCA Civ 785, [2008] 2 P.&C.R. 24 the Court of Appeal approved the statement in the text that the Court adopts a cautious approach. In that case they reversed the decision of the judge at first instance to order a transfer of the property and substituted an order for reimbursement of expenditure.

NOTE 46. ADD: In *Wormall v Wormall* [2004] EWCA Civ 1643 E claimed possession of business premises which he had permitted his daughter, C, to occupy for the foreseeable future for the purpose of her business but now wished to sell because of his divorce. The judge at first instance held that E was estopped from claiming possession until the ancillary relief order was made and awarded C compensation for the future loss of occupation. The Court of Appeal allowed E's appeal against that part of the order on the basis that the minimum equity to do justice between the parties was to permit C to occupy the premises until the divorce proceedings were concluded. See also *Clark v Clark* [2006] EWHC 275 (Ch), [2006] W.T.L.R. 823 in which the relief granted by Blackburne J was to dismiss (in part) a claim for possession.

NOTE 25. ADD: In *Cobbe v Yeomans Row Management Ltd* [2005] EWHC **10–25**
266 (Ch) the Court awarded a charge over a development property for
half the increase in its value due to the grant of planning permission.
For the facts see para.10–20, note 18.

NOTE 65. ADD: For discussion of *Holiday Inns Inc v Broadhead* see now **10–26**
Yeoman's Row Management Ltd v Cobbe [2008] UKHL 55, [2008] 1 W.L.R.
1752 at [24] (Lord Scott) and [76] to [78] (Lord Walker) referred to in
paragraph 10–19, note 2 above.

NOTE 77. ADD: In *Lloyd v Sutcliffe* [2008] EWHC 1329 (Ch) Norris J. **10–27**
made an award of £25,000 in order to satisfy the equity. He held that
relevant factors included the nature of the expectation created by the
defendant, the detriment suffered by the claimant in reliance on those
representations, the degree to which the defendant's conduct could
properly be said to be unconscionable, and the need for some proportionality between the claimant's expectation and his or her detriment.
The claimant's only expectation had been to participate in any profit
yielded by the development. The defendant had deprived him of that
expectation and had relieved him of that obligation. Since he did not
have to build at cost, the detriment that he had suffered had been to
devote his time and skills and to deploy his knowledge and connection
in promoting the company's development rather than his own individual project. He also held (following the Court of Appeal's decision at
[2007] EWCA Civ 153, [2007] E.G. 162 on an appeal against an ealier
judgment of his) that it would be just to require the claimant to look first
to the company, which had been the expected source of his profit share.

4.   Effect on third parties

NOTE 85. ADD: For consideration of the continuing liability of the repres- **10–28**
entor see Bright and McFarlane "Personal Liabiilty in Proprietary
Estoppel" [2005] 69 Conv. 14.

CHAPTER 11

PENALTIES AND FOFEITURES

1. CONTRAST BETWEEN PENALTIES AND FORFEITURE

NOTE 1. ADD: For a detailed historical study of the earliest form of **11–1** penalties see Biancalana "Contractual Penalties in the King's Court 1260–1360" [2005] 64 C.L.J. 212–242.

2. PENALTIES

1. Nature of a penalty

ADD NEW PARAGRAPH: In *Murray v Leisureplay Plc* [2005] EWCA Civ 963 C **11–4A** was dismissed as a director of D. Under the terms of his contract C was entitled to a payment of 1 year's salary for loss of office. D argued that this was a penalty. The judge held at first instance that it was because it failed to take into account C's duty to mitigate. Each of the judgments contain a useful summary of the relevant principles. See Arden L.J. at [29] to [54], Clarke L.J. at [106] and Buxton L.J. at [109] to [111]. All of the judgments emphasise the fact that the stipulated sum must be compensatory rather an deterrent and all emphasised the importance of contractual certainty in this context. The stipulated sum must be so extravagant to be unconscionable before the Court will refuse to enforce it.

NOTE 13. ADD: In *M&J Polymers Ltd v Imerys Minerals Ltd* [2008] EWHC **11–4** 344 (Comm), [2008] 1 All E.R. (Comm) 893, Burton J. applied the principle stated in the text to a "pay and pay clause" (i.e. a clause which required a purchaser to pay for a minimum quantity of goods even if the purchaser had not ordered them). However, he was able to construe the relevant provision as applying on breach: see [39] to [44]. Although he held that the doctrine applied, he held that the clause was not a penalty because it was commercially justifiable, it did not amount to oppression, was negotiated and freely entered by the parties and did not have the predominant purpose of deterring a breach: see [46].

2 PENALTIES

2. Relief in equity

NOTE 22. ADD: For a detailed historical study of the earliest form of **11–5** penalties see Biancalana "Contractual Penalties in the King's Court 1260–1360" [2005] 64 C.L.J. 212–242. Biancalana locates the origins of penalties in a much earlier period than has historically been recognised in earlier versions of this work.

3. Penalties distinguished from liquidated damages

11–10 The decision of Stanley Burnton J. in *Murray v Leisureplay* was reversed by the CA: see [2005] EWCA Civ 963, [2005] I.R.L.R. 946. For comment on the decision see Dharmananda & Vinjeich *Reinventing the Wheel: Recent Interpretation of Dunlop in the Penalty Doctrine* [2006] L.M.C.L.Q. 154.

2. RELIEF AGAINST FORFEITURE

3. Contracts for the Sale of Land

11–20 NOTE 83. ADD: In *Aribisala v St James Homes (Grosvenor Dock) Ltd* [2007] EWHC 1694 (Ch), 2007 3 E.G.L.R. 39 it was held that it was not possible to exclude the operation of section 49(2) by agreement.

NOTE 84. ADD: In *Midill (97PL) Ltd v Park Lane Estates Ltd* [2009] EWCA Civ 1227, [2009] 2 All E.R. 1067, [2009] 1 E.G.L.R. 65 Carnwath L.J. reviewed all of the authorities and academic comment on section 49(2) and concluded (at [52]) that the jurisdiction remained exceptional. On the facts, the Court found that the purchaser was not entitled to the return of its deposit although the vendor had resold the property at a profit.

NOTE 85. ADD: In the subsequent hearing to determine whether the deposit should be returned (*Aribisala v St James Homes (Grosvenor Dock) Ltd* [2008] EWHC 456 (Ch), [2008] 3 All E.R. 762) Floyd J held that it was insufficient to justify the return of a deposit that the vendor had made a significant profit from the breach of contract although the effect on the vendor was one factor to be taken into account. He stated the relevant considerations at [13] as follows: "I think what needs to be looked at is how close the purchaser came to performing the contract, what alternatives he was able to propose to the vendor and how advantageous they would be compared with actual performance of the contractual terms. Where the purchaser simply could not perform the contract or offer any such alternative, then it would be exceptional, as Arden L.J. held, for the deposit to be returned."

PART IV

EQUITABLE REMEDIES

Chapter 13

RESCISSION

2 Relation to Other Rules of Contract

1. mistake

ADD THE FOLLOWING AT THE BEGINNING OF THE PARAGRAPH: There are only **13–2** limited circumstances in which a transaction may be challenged in equity on the grounds of mistake. Unilateral transactions may be challenged on the grounds of mistake, whether the cause of the mistake was fraud, undue influence, misrepresentation or simple mistake: but where the basis of challenging the transaction is simple mistake, it is necessary to establish that the transaction was not merely unilateral but voluntary [NOTE 1A], and that the mistake was of so serious a character as to render it unjust on the part of the donee to retain the property [NOTE 1B]. It has been held that the mistake must be a mistake as to the effect of the transaction itself and not merely to its consequences or the advantages to be gained by entering into it [NOTE 1C]: if this is correct [NOTE 1D], then a misapprehension as to the consequences (including the tax consequences) of a unilateral transaction will not be relevant [NOTE 1E]. The position is different in respect of other transactions.

ADD NEW NOTE 1A: See *Smithson v Hamilton* [2007] EWHC 2900 (Ch), applying *Gibbon v Mitchell* [1990] 1 W.L.R. 1304. A suggestion that the principle has a wider application (supported by dicta in *A.M.P. v Barker* [2001] P.L.R. 77 and *Gallagher Ltd v Gallagher Pensions Ltd* [2005] EWHC 42 (Ch)) was rejected on the basis that those dicta had been superseded by *Great Peace Shipping Ltd v Tsavlaris Salvage (International) Ltd* [2002] EWCA Civ 1407: see [2007] EWHC 2900 (Ch), at [110]–[119].

ADD NEW NOTE 1B: See *Ogilvie v Littleboy* (1897) 13 T.L.R. 399, at 400 per Lindley L.J.; affirmed *sub nom. Ogilvie v Allen* (1899) 15 T.L.R. 294. See also *Sieff v Fox* [2005] EWHC 1312 (Ch), paras.[99]–[100].

ADD NEW NOTE 1C: See *Gibbon v Mitchell* [1990] 1 W.L.R. 1304, at 1309 per Millett J.; also *Anker-Petersen v Christiensen* [2002] W.T.L.R. 313 and *Wolff v Wolff* [2004] EWHC 2110 (Ch). Since the effect of a transaction includes its indirect effect (see *Ellis v Ellis* (1909) 26 T.L.R. 166), the distinction between effect and consequences may not be an easy one to draw: see *Sieff v Fox* [2005] EWHC 1312 (Ch) at paras.[95], [102] and [104]–[105].

ADD NEW NOTE 1D: The scope of the proposition is uncertain since, as explained by Lloyd L.J. in *Sieff v Fox* [2005] EWHC 1312 (Ch), there is no decided case directly on point: *loc cit*, para.[106]. The proposition does not apply where a trustee mistakenly disposes of trust assets, since that case is governed by the rule in *Re Hastings-Bass*: see para.9–09 ff above. In *Sieff v Fox*, although expressing some doubts about the correctness of the proposition, Lloyd LJ was content to proceed on the basis that the proposition applied in cases where the transaction is by an individual disposing of his/her own assets: *ibid*, at paras.[106] and [108]. See also (2006) 122 L.Q.R. 35 (Mitchell).

ADD NEW NOTE 1E: See *Anker-Petersen v Christiensen* [2002] W.T.L.R. 313, at 330–31 *per* Davis J.

NOTE 2: ADD: For the view that there may still be an equitable jurisdiction to grant rescission on the basis of a unilateral (as opposed to a common) mistake, see [2005] L.Q.R. 393 (Yeo).

3   GROUND FOR RECISSION

4. Constructive fraud

13–11 ADD: A transaction may also be set aside where one of the parties, although aware that his agent has accepted (or agreed to accept) a bribe, has not given his informed consent to such action [NOTE 51A]

ADD NEW NOTE 51A: See *Wilson v Hurstanger Ltd* [2007] EWCA Civ 299 at [47]–[51] (Tuckey LJ); also *Ross River Ltd v Cambridge City Football Club Ltd* [2007] EWHC 2115 (Ch) at [203]–[205].

4   RECISSION—AN ACT OF THE INNOCENT PARTY, OR AN ACT OF THE COURT?

13–13 NOTE 54: ADD: For a contrary view, see Poole and Keyser (2005) 121 L.Q.R. 273, at 284–89. The question was raised (at first instance) in *Halpern v Halpern (No.2)* [2006] EWHC 1728 (Comm), but no view expressed: *ibid*, paras.[27]–[28].

NOTE 56:   ADD: For a discussion of the limitations of the common law (particularly in cases where title to property has passed) see Swadling (2005) 121 L.Q.R. 123.

5   LOSS OF RIGHT OF RECISSION

1. By acquiescence

13–16 NOTE 61: ADD: Where the claimant's ignorance is sufficient to defeat a defence of express (or constructive) waiver, a defence based on acquiescence (or estoppel) may still succeed: see *Habib Bank Ltd v Tufail* [2006] EWCA Civ 374, at para.[20].

13–17

2. By impossibility of restitutio in integrum

NOTE 64; ADD: The primary objective may not always need to be to restore *both* parties to their previous positions, however: see *Halpern v Halpern (No.2)* [2007] EWCA Civ 291, at [74] per Carnwath L.J.

NOTE 67: DELETE FINAL SENTENCE AND ADD: The Court's ability to make a monetary order in lieu of rescission has been recognised by the Court of Appeal on several occasions: see *O'Sullivan v Management Agency and Music Ltd* [1985] 1 Q.B. 428 (CA); also *Halpern v Halpern (No.2)* [2007] EWCA Civ 291, at [60] per Carnwath LJ. However, it does not follow that *restitutio in integrum* is to be treated as always being possible; whether restitution is possible is a question of fact and degree in each case: *ibid*, at [75].

6   EFFECT OF RECISSION

1. Recission of entire transactions

NOTE 87: ADD: See also Poole and Keyser (2005) 121 L.Q.R. 273.   **13–21**

CHAPTER 14

RECTIFICATION

1 NATURE OF RECTIFICATION

1. The remedy

DELETE FINAL SENTENCE, AND INSERT: The purpose of interpretation is not to **14–01** identify the literal meaning of the words that the parties have used; but, rather, to identify what the parties to the transaction meant when they used the words that they did.

It follows that, although the starting point must be the words of the instrument [NOTE 1A], the Court may conclude that something has gone wrong in reducing the parties agreement to writing. Such a conclusion may be justified by the express terms of the instrument itself: eg, where the language does not make grammatical sense [NOTE 1B]; or the language is ambiguous [NOTE 1C]; or where the instrument uses what appears to be a technical term without providing a definition [NOTE 1D]. Such a conclusion may also be justified by reference to the objectively ascertained facts surrounding the conclusion of the agreement: eg where it would be obvious to a reasonable person with the relevant background knowledge that there was a mistake in the language of the instrument [NOTE 1E]; or where the terms of an instrument appear to be contrary to commercial common sense [NOTE 1F]. Although the language of the instrument and at least some "surrounding circumstances" may be taken into account when considering whether something has gone wrong in reducing the agreement to writing, the current state of the law is that pre-contractual negotiations between the parties (which, by their nature, were intended to be superseded by the written instrument) are irrelevant at this part of the inquiry [NOTE 1G].

If the Court is satisfied that something has gone wrong in reducing the agreement to writing, it will be able to correct the error as a matter of construction if - and only if - it is clear what correction ought to be made in order to cure the mistake [NOTE 1H]. In considering whether it is clear how the error should be corrected, the court is entitled to have regard both to the language of the instrument and the surrounding circumstances. Those circumstances will include matters which were known to both the parties, as well as prior agreements to which they were party [NOTE 1I]; but evidence of pre-contractual negotiations is admissible only where they demonstrate a clear concensus on the point at issue [NOTE 1J]. Where the correction involves interpolating words, the task will be easier if the precise words to be inserted appear on the evidence [NOTE 1K]; but it will be sufficient if the evidence identifies the gist of the words to be inserted [NOTE 1L].

INSERT NEW NOTES 1A to AL, as follows:

NOTE 1A: See e.g. *B.C.C.I. v Ali* [2001] UKHL 8, at [8] (Lord Bingham) and at [37]–[39] (Lord Hoffmann); *Melanesian Mission Trust Board v Australian Mutual Provident Society* [1996] UKPC 53; also *J.I.S. (1974) Ltd v M.C.P. Investment Nominees Ltd* [2003] EWCA Civ 721, at [10] (Carnwath LJ); *Holding & Barnes plc v Hill House Hammond Ltd* [2001] EWCA Civ 1334, at [14]–[18] (Clarke LJ).

NOTE 1B: See *Homburg Houtimport B.V. v Agrosin Private Ltd* [2003] UKHL 13, at [23] (Lord Bingham).

NOTE 1C: See *Investors Compensation Scheme Ltd v West Bromwich B.S.* [1998] 1 W.L.R. 896 (H.L.), at 912–13 (Lord Hoffmann's third principle); *The Karen Oltmann* [1976] 2 Lloyd's Rep. 708 (Kerr J) (meaning of word "after").

NOTE 1D: See *Proforce Recruit Ltd v The Rugby Group Ltd* [2006] EWCA Civ 69 (meaning of expression "preferred supplier status").

NOTE 1E: See *Investors Compensation Scheme Ltd v West Bromwich B.S.* [1998] 1 W.L.R. 896 (H.L.), at 912–13 (Lord Hoffmann's third principle); also *East v Pantiles Plant Hire Ltd* [1982] 2 E.G.L.R. 111 (CA), at 112 (Brightman LJ); *Holding & Barnes Plc v Hill House Hammond Ltd* [2001] EWCA Civ 1334, at [21] (Clarke LJ).

NOTE 1F: See *Investors Compensation Scheme Ltd v West Bromwich B.S.* [1998] 1 W.L.R. 896 (H.L.), at 912–13 (Lord Hoffmann's fifth principle); also *Antaios Compania Naviera S.A. v Salen Rederierna A.B.* [1985] A.C. 191, at 201 (Lord Diplock); *Law Land Co Ltd v Consumers Association Ltd* [1980] 2 E.G.L.R. 109, at 111B-C (Brightman L.J.). See also *Holding & Barnes Plc v Hill House Hammond Ltd* (above). Such an approach is only permissible where the terms of- the instrument will bear a purposive construction: see *Equity & Law Life Assurance Society v Bodfield Ltd* [1987] 1 E.G.L.R. 124, at 125F-H (Dillon L.J.).

NOTE 1G: See *Prenn v Simmonds* [1971] 1 W.L.R. 1381 (H.L.), at [xxx] *per* Lord Wilberforce; *Investors Compensation Scheme Ltd v West Bromwich B.S.* [1998] 1 W.L.R. 896 (H.L.), at 912–13 (Lord Hoffmann's third principle); *The Rio Assu (No.2)* [1999] 1 Lloyd's Rep. 115 (C.A.), at 124 (Waller LJ); *Alexiou v Campbell* [2007] UKPC 11, at [15] (Lord Bingham); *Chartbrook v Persimmon Homes Ltd* [2008] EWCA Civ 183, at [105] (Lawrence Collins L.J.), [187] (Rimer L.J.) and [191] (Tuckey L.J.). For the possibility of future changes in the law, see e.g. *Chartbrook v Persimmon Homes Ltd* above, at [108]–[113]. See also *The Interpretation of Contracts* (Lewison) (4th Ed, 2007), at 69–78.

NOTE 1H: *Homburg Houtimport B.V. v Agrosin Private Ltd* [2003] UKHL 13, at [23] (Lord Bingham) and [192] (Lord Millett); *East v Pantiles Plant*

Hire Ltd [1982] 2 E.G.L.R. 111 (CA), at 112 (Brightman LJ); *Holding & Barnes Plc v Hill House Hammond Ltd* [2001] EWCA Civ 1334. See also paragraph 14–17 below

NOTE 1I: See *H.I.H. Casulalty and General Assurance Ltd v New Hampshire Insurance Co* [2001] EWCA Civ 735, at [82]–[84] (Rix L.J.). Although an earlier agreement may be admissible, the court may be left not knowing what significance to attach to it (especially if the later instrument was intended to supersede the earlier agreement): *ibid*; but see *KPMG v Network Rail Infrastructure Ltd* [2007] EWCA Civ 363 where weight was given to the words of an earlier agreement even though (objectively speaking) the term in question had been renegotiated.

NOTE 1J: See *The Karen Oltmann* [1976] 2 Lloyd's Rep. 708 (meaning of the word "after" identified by reference to the way the parties had used the word in their pre-contractual exchanges); *Proforce Recruit v The Rugby Group Ltd* [2006] EWCA Civ 69, at [31] (Mummery L.J.) and [55] (Arden L.J.). However, evidence of an agreed meaning will not be admissible in a case where the clear terms of the instrument preclude this (e.g. where the expression in question is expressly defined in the instrument itself): see *Chartbrook Ltd v Persimmon Homes Ltd* [2008] EWCA Civ 183, at [187] (Rimer L.J.) and [192] (Tuckey L.J.).

NOTE 1K: "I take it to be clear in principle that the court should not interpolate words into a written instrument, of whatever nature, unless it is clear both that words have been omitted *and what those omitted words were. . .* ": *Homburg Houtimport BV v Agrosin Private Ltd* [2003] UKHL 13, at [23] *per* Lord Bingham (emphasis supplied).

NOTE 1L: "Where [the court] can see, not only that words have been omitted, but what those words are, then it is its duty to supply them. It is not necessary that the court should be certain precisely what words have been omitted; it is sufficient that it knows their gist": *Homburg Houtimport BV v Agrosin Private Ltd* [2003] UKHL 13, at [192] *per* Lord Millett. This passage from Lord Millett's speech may produce difficulties in cases where the gist of the parties' intention is only known at a relatively high degree of generality; so that there are several forms of words that might properly be said to express the gist of their intention. The difficulties arise because (in relation to cases where two or more materially different forms of words might be said to achieve the gist of what was agreed) Lord Millett did not identify any criteria by which to identify the form of words that should be inserted. This problem arose for consideration in *KPMG v Network Rail Infrastructure Ltd* [2007] EWCA Civ 363 where (although unable to identify the common intention of the parties in the context of a claim for rectification) the court felt able to choose between two materially different forms of words as a matter of interpretation: see [65]–[67]; *sed quaere*.

(c)   *Rectification as a qualification to the parole evidence rule:*

14–3   ADD, AFTER THE REFERENCE TO NOTE 5: In some cases rectification (by supplementing its terms) may give effect to an instrument which might otherwise be void [NOTE 5A].

NOTE 5: REPLACE WITH THE FOLLOWING: See paras 14–10 to 14–12 below.

INSERT NEW NOTE 5A: Thus rectification may be available in respect of a contract to which section 2 of the Law of Property (Miscellaneous Provisions) Act 1989 applies, even though (i) the written document (prior to rectification) does not contain the true terms of the agreement and (ii) the accord which supports the claim to rectification is not a contract. The availability of this remedy is expressly recognised by section 2(4) of the 1989 Act, which provides that a contract satisfying the requirements of section 2 by reason only of the rectification of one or more documents in pursuance of an order of the court will come into being (or be deemed to come into being) at such time as may be specified in the order. Although the process of rectification in this context is an unusual form of rectification (since it does not necessarily have retrospective effect), the availability of the remedy is to be judged by reference to the usual rules: see *Oun v Ahmad* [2008] EWHC 545 (Ch) at [38] (Morgan J.).

3   CONDITIONS TO BE SATISFIED

2. Mistake

(a)   Common Mistake

14–14   NOTE 51: DELETE THE ENTIRE NOTE, AND ADD: See *Joscelyne v Nissen* above, at 98. L.J. Bromley has suggested that there should be no requirement to establish an outward expression of accord: see (1971) 87 L.Q.R. 532; criticised by M. Smith at (2007) L.Q.R. 116. It has also been suggested that the requirement is a practical (ie an evidential) one, rather than a strict legal requirement: see *Munt v Beasley* [2006] EWCA Civ 370, at [36] per Mummery L.J. There is a considerable degree of inter-action between this requirement and the requirement, in order to obtain an order for rectification, to establish that on a particular point the instrument fails to reflect the parties' accord on that point (see note 50 above). No outward manifestation of the parties' accord is required in cases where the instrument is not intended to set out an accord between two or more parties (ie, if the underlying transaction is unilateral - see paragraph 14–15 below); nor where a unilateral transaction requires the consent of another: *AMP (UK) Plc v Barker* [2001] Pens.L.R. 77; followed in *Gallaher Ltd v Gallaher Pensions Ltd and others* [2005] EWHC 42 (Ch).

NOTE 78: ADD: See also para.13–02 above.

(b)   Unilateral mistake

14–15   NOTE 82: ADD: The mistake must be that of the principal: see *George Wimpey UK Ltd v V.I. Construction Ltd* [2005] EWCA Civ 77, at [48]–[50].

NOTE 90: ADD: See also *Littman v Aspen Oil (Broking) Ltd* [2005] EWCA Civ 1579.

NOTE 92: ADD: Buckley LJ's formulation of those conditions has been accepted as being authoritative: see *George Wimpey UK Ltd v V.I. Construction Ltd* [2005] EWCA Civ 77, at paras [38], [52] and [68]. For a slightly different formulation, however, see *Hurst Stores and Interiors Ltd v ML Europe Property Ltd* [2004] EWCA Civ 490, at [20].

NOTE 93: ADD: See also *Hurst Stores and Interiors Ltd v ML Europe Property Ltd* [2004] EWCA Civ 490, at [19]–[20].

3.   Absence of alternative remedy

(a)   Adequacy of the common law

AFTER THE REFERENCE TO NOTE 6, ADD: Similarly, "in the case of notice given **14–17** by the landlord" may be construed as meaning "in the case of notice given by the tenant" [NOTE 16A].

DELETE THE SENTENCE IMMEDIATE BEFORE THE REFERENCE TO NOTE 19, AND REPLACE WITH: If the material which it is sought (by rectification) to insert in the written instrument is already enforceable as a collateral contract, then specific performance of that collateral contract will be granted and rectification of the instrument will be refused [NOTE 19].

NOTE 9: ADD: A more recent formulation of the principle is to be found in the judgment of Brightman L.J. in *East v Pantiles Plant Hire Ltd* [1982] 2 E.G.L.R. 111 (CA), at 112A, which has been adopted by the Court of Appeal in *Holding & Barnes Plc v Hill House Hammond Ltd* [2001] EWCA Civ 1334. See also *Homburg Houtimport BV v Agrosin Ltd* [2003] UKHL 12, at [23] (Lord Bingham), [94] (Lord Hoffmann) and [192] (Lord Millett). See para 14–01 above.

ADD NEW NOTE 16A: *Littman v Aspen Oil (Broking) Ltd* [2005] EWHC 1369 (Ch), affirmed [2005] EWCA Civ 1579.

NOTE 17: ADD: But see *KPMG v Network Rail Infrastructure Ltd* [2007] EWCA Civ 363, at [65]–[67]; also para 14–01 above.

4   DEFENCES

1.   Valid defences

ADD TO THE END OF THE TEXT: Performance of the contract will not always **14–19** amount to a defence, however, at least where the performance was monetary and it is arguable that it (or part of it) is repayable on restitutionary grounds [note 27a]. An order for rectification will also be refused where the parties have already varied their agreement so as to correct the error, so that the only consequence of the court's order would be to secure a fiscal benefit [note 27b].

ADD NOTE 27A: *The Toronto Dominion Bank v Oberoi and others* [2003] EWHC 3216.

ADD NOTE 27B: See *Racal Group Services Ltd v Ashmore* [1995] S.T.C. 1151, and para.14–20 below

14–20   DELETE THE THIRD SENTENCE (WHICH REFERS TO FOOTNOTES 36 AND 37) AND REPLACE WITH THE FOLLOWING: Provided that the court is otherwise satisfied that rectification should be granted (ie, it is satisfied that a document does not give effect to the true agreement or arrangement between the parties, or to the true intention of a grantor or covenantor; and if satisfied that there is an issue, capable of being contested between the parties or between a covenantor or a grantor and the person he intended to benefit), it is irrelevant first that the rectification of the document is sought or consented to by all of the parties, and second that rectification is desired because it has beneficial fiscal consequences [NOTE 36]. On the other hand, the court will not order rectification of a document as between the parties or as between a grantor or covenantor and an intended beneficiary, if their rights will be unaffected and if the only effect of the order will be to secure a fiscal advantage [NOTE 37].

REPLACE NOTE 36 WITH THE FOLLOWING: See *Racal Group Services Ltd v Ashmore* [1995] S.T.C. 1151 (CA) at 1157 (Peter Gibson L.J.), approving a passage from the judgment of Vinelott J. at first instance [1995] S.T.C. 416, at 425. See also *Re Colebrook's Conveyances* [1972] 1 W.L.R. 1397; *Re Slocock's Will Trusts* [1979] 1 All E.R. 358, and *Lake v Lake* [1989] S.T.C. 865.

REPLACE NOTE 37 AS FOLLOWS: See *Whiteside v Whiteside* [1950] Ch 65 (CA), where the parties had already entered into a supplementary deed rectifying the error before the matter came to court. See also *Racal Group Services Ltd v Ashmore* [1995] S.T.C. 1151, at 1158 per Peter Gibson L.J.

5   EFFECT OF ORDER

1. Form of order

14–21   NOTE 44: ADD: If an instrument sets out the basis on which a thing is to be valued, and one party asserts that the instrument should be rectified so as to set out a different (or modified) basis of valuation, it may be tempting for the valuer to rely upon *Law v Warren* as justifying the production of one valuation based on the instrument as executed; but there is frequently much to be said for the valuer's proceeding to value on each of the two alternative bases (but identifying the basis which the valuer prefers) with a view to leaving the parties then to decide how to proceed: see *Simmers v Innes* [2008] UKHL 24, at [31] per Lord Neuberger.

CHAPTER 15

SPECIFIC PERFORMANCE

ADD THE FOLLOWING AT THE END OF THE FIRST PARAGRAPH OF SECTION (2) **15–34** ("SLIGHT MISDESCRIPTION"): In such cases it is possible that the vendor is entitled to require completion to take place [5a]; but because the purchaser is entitled to be compensated by way of an abatement to the purchase price the vendor is not entitled to require payment of the full (unabated) price as a condition of completion [5b].

ADD NEW NOTE 5A: The position is far from certain. In *Johns v Deacon* [1985] C.A.T. 13, the vendor contracted to sell land which included a fixture, but disposed of that fixture prior to completion; the Court of Appeal held that a notice to complete which required completion at the full price was invalid, and observed that no valid notice to complete could be given until the amount by which the purchase price was to be abated had been agreed or determined. In *Bechal v Kitsford Holdings Ltd* [1989] 1 W.L.R. 105, there was a misdescription as to the size of the land to be conveyed; Brown-Wilkinson V-C (who had been a member of the Court in the *Johns* case) held that the misdescription entitled the purchaser to an abatement of the purchase price but did not invalidate the vendor's notice to complete. In *Clowes Development Ltd v Mulchinock* [1998] 1 W.L.R. 42, Carnwath J. attempted to reconcile the two cases: *loc cit*, at pp.49–50. In *Donnelly v Weybridge Construction Ltd* [2006] EWHC 2678 (TCC), at [238], Ramsey J. preferred the view expressed in *Johns v Deacon*.

ADD NEW NOTE 5B: *Johns v Deacon* [1985] C.A.T. 13; *Donnelly v Weybridge Construction Ltd* [2006] EWHC 2678 (TCC).

INSERT, AFTER THE REFERENCE TO NOTE 63: The period of delay which will **15–38** bar a claim to specific performance is to be judged by such equitable principles, and not by analogy with section 5 of the Limitation Act 1980 [NOTE 64].

NOTE 62: ADD: Any suggestion that a claimant can delay for years in bringing his suit for specific performance is therefore contrary to well-established principle: see *P & O Nedlloyd B.V. v Arab Metals Co.* [2006] EWCA Civ 1717, at [50] per Moore-Bick LJ.

ADD NEW NOTE 64: If a statutory limitation provision (properly interpreted) applies to a claim, then equity will apply it in obedience to the statute; and even where the limitation period does not apply to the claim (because the claim is for an exclusively equitable remedy) the limitation will be applied by analogy if the equitable remedy is "correspondent to the remedy at law": see *P & O Nedlloyd B.V. v Arab Metals Co.* [2006] EWCA Civ 1717, at [34]–[38] per Moore-Bick LJ. However, the remedy of specific performance is not correspondent to any common law remedy; so that no period of limitation applies by analogy: *ibid*, at [44]–[52] per Moore-Bick LJ. Whether a statutory period of limitation should be applied by analogy to claims for monetary relief in lieu of specific performance remains uncertain.

CHAPTER 16

INJUNCTION

NOTE 49: ADD: It is for this reason that the court may restrain the ower of **16–8** a ship from acting with its commitments under a time charter, even though (being a contract for services) the charter would not be specifically performed: see *Lady Navigation Inc v Lauritzencool AB* [2005] EWCA Civ 579 at paras. [8]–[20], explaining *Scadanavian Trading Tanker Co AB v Flota Petrolera Ecuatoriana (The Scaptrade)* [1983] 2 A.C. 694; see also (2005) 121 L.Q.R. 560 (Devonshire).

NOTE 58. ADD: The position is otherwise where the contract is not for personal services but is, rather, a commercial arrangement which involves the employment of unnamed individuals: *Lady Navigation Inc v Lauritzencool AB* [2005] EWCA Civ 579.

NOTE 19: ADD: The court's jurisdiction under this section is limited, and **16–9** does not extend to every order that might be intended to prevent a continuation of a breach of the criminal law: *Worcester CC v Tongue* [2004] EWCA Civ 140.

NOTE 43: ADD: Provided that the defendant has been put on notice of **16–14** the claim but decides to proceed with the works nevertheless, this is so whether the claimant (i) fails to obtain interim relief, or (ii) does not seek interim relief: see *Mortimer v Bailey* [2004] EWCA Civ 1514, noted at [2005] Conv. 460 (Watt). Where the defendant's right to carry out works is in doubt, the prudent course is to seek an adjudication (or agreement) on those rights before works are undertaken: *Mortimer v Bailey* at [41].

NOTE 48: ADD: See also *Crestfort Ltd v Tesco Stores Ltd and another* [2005] EWHC 805 (Ch) at [57] and [69]–[70], where the matter is given fuller analysis.

NOTE 55: ADD: It would seem that some interferences with a right may **16–15** be sufficiently material to constitute a nuisance, without being sufficiently material to justify the grant of an injunction: see *Midtown Ltd v City of London Real Property Co Ltd* [2005] EWHC 33 (Ch) at [79].

ADD TO MAIN TEXT AFTER NOTE 78: All such precedents are cases on the **16–16** exercise of a discretion, so that none is binding: the most they demonstrate is that in similar circumstances it would not be wrong to exercise the discretion in the same way.[NOTE 78a].

ADD TO MAIN TEXT AFTER NOTE 95: or that the defendant's conduct, although reprehensible, is not sufficiently connected to the claim under consideration [NOTE 95a].

ADD TO MAIN TEXT AFTER NOTE 96: Nor, in cases where a mandatory injunction is sought to restore the status quo ante, will an injunction be refused merely on the ground that the claimant did not obtain interim relief. [NOTE 96a].

ADD NEW NOTE 78A: *Jaggard v Sawyer* [1995] 1 W.L.R. 269, at 288A (Millett L.J.). See also *Midtown Ltd v City of London Real Property Co Ltd* [2005] EWHC 33 (Ch), at [73]–[75].

NOTE 84: ADD: But, where a contract imposes both positive and negative obligations, the court may restrain a breach of the negative obligations even though it would not decree specific performance of the positive obligations: see para.16–08 above (note 49).

NOTE 88: ADD: See also J. Willis & Son v Willis [1986] 1 E.G.L.R. 62, and *Gonthier v Orange Contract Scaffolding Ltd* [2003] EWCA Civ 873.

NOTE 92: ADD: The court should be astute to detect claims for injunction which are made by people whose real interest in their rights is monetary, and who seek injunctive relief in order to secure a negotiating advantage over the defendant: see *Midtown Ltd v City of London Real Property Co Ltd* [2005] EWHC 33 (Ch), at [70]–[80].

ADD NEW NOTE 95A: The misconduct must have "an immediate and necessary relation to the equity sued for": *Dering v Earl of Winchelsea* (1787) 1 Cox 318 at 319–20 *per* Eyre CB; *Moody v Cox* [1917] 2 Ch 71, at 87; *Memory Corporation plc v Sidhu* [2000] 1 W.L.R. 1443, at 1457. Conduct in the course of litigation which has no bearing on the substantive rights of the parties will not have the necessary degree of connexion: *Fiona Trust & Holding Corporation v Privalov* [2008] EWHC 1748 (Comm), at [23]–[26].

ADD NEW NOTE 96a: See *Mortimer v Bailey* [2004] EWCA Civ 1514, where the defendant carried out works in knowledge of the claimant's intention to seek a final injunction, even though an interim injunction had been refused. See also para.16–14.

NOTE 3: ADD: For two examples, where the question of conscionability was considered on the facts, see *Gafford v Graham* [1999] 3 E.G.L.R. 75 (acquiescence), and *Harris v Williams-Wynne* [2006] EWCA Civ 104 (no acquiescence): the distinction between the facts of the two cases is usefully identified in *Harris* at paragraphs [36]–[39] (Chadwick L.J.). See also para.18–11.

16–19   SUBSTITUTE NEW PARAGRAPH: The power of a judge sitting in the High Court to grant an injunction against a party to proceedings properly served arises out of the court's inherent jurisdiction, as confirmed by statute [NOTE 15]. The terms of the statute are expressed in wide terms, providing that the court may grant such injunctions "where it appears to the court to be just and convenient so to do". However, as a matter of settled practice the court will only exercise that jurisdiction in limited circumstances [NOTE 16]. In particular, the right to an interim injunction cannot exist in isolation, but is always incidental to and dependant upon the enforcement of a substantive right which usually (although not invariably) takes the shape of a cause of action [NOTE 17].

SUBSTITUTE NEW NOTE 15: See *Fourie v Le Roux* [2007] UKHL 1, at [25] (Lord Scott), [1], [5], [44] and [47]. The High Court's jurisdiction is currently confirmed by the Supreme Court Act 1981, s.37(1). The statutory forebears of s.37(1) were the Supreme Court of Judicature Act 1873 s.25(8), and the Supreme Court of Judicature (Consolidation) Act 1925, s.45(1). Those statutory provisions confirm the High Court's existing jurisdiciton, as appears from s.16 of the 1873 Act and s.19(2)(b) of the 1981 Act. The court also has a statutory jurisdiciton in aid of foreign proceedings, and in aid of arbitrations. It may grant interim relief in respect of proceedings on foot in another state which is either a party to the Brussels or Lugano Conventions, or which is a Regulation State within the meaning of s.25(1) the Civil Jurisdiction and Judgments Act 1982 (as amended), provided that two conditions are satisfied. The first condition is that the foreign claim must be such that the relief sought in England can be identified as interim relief in relation to the final order sought abroad in the proceedings relied on: *Fourie v Le Roux and others* [2007] UKHL 1 at [31]. The second condition is that there must be a real connecting link between the relief sought and the English court's territorial jurisdiction: *Van Uden Maritime BV v KG Deco-Line* [1999] Q.B. 1225. In relation to arbitrations governed by the Arbitration Act 1996, the court has power (unless the parties agree otherwise) to grant interim injunctions (see Arbitration Act 1996, s.44(1) & 44(2). Applications under Arbitration Act 1996 s.44 must normally be made on notice; but in urgent cases an application for a freezing order or search order may be made *ex parte*: Arbitration Act 1996, sections 44(4) and 44(3); *Cetelem S.A. v Roust Holdings Ltd.*

NOTE 16: These limitations are as to the exercise of the court's jurisdiction rather than its extent: see *Fourie v Le Roux* [2007] UKHL 1 at [25] and [30]; also *Albon (t/a NA Carriage Co) v Naza Motor Trading Sdn Bhd* [2007] EWCA Civ 1124 at [7].

NOTE 17: ADD: In respect of a cause of action arising within England and Wales, it would be difficult to justify the grant of interim injunctive relief without the issue of substantive proceedings or an undertaking to do so: *Fourie v Le Roux* [2007] UKHL 1, at [32]. Consequently, whenever an interlocutiry injunction is applied for, the judge (if otherwise minded to grant the order) should, as a matter of good practice, pay careful attention to the substantive relief that is (or will be) sought: *Fourie*, at [33].

ADD REFERENCE TO NEW NOTE 17A AFTER FIRST SENTENCE OF MAIN TEXT. **16–20**

ADD NEW NOTE 17a: Provided that the defendant exists, it is not necessary that he/she be identified. Accordingly, an injunction may be granted against persons unknown: *South Cambridgeshire DC v Persons*

Unknown [2004] EWCA Civ 1280, approving *Bloomsbury Publishing plc v Newsgroup Newspapers Ltd* [2003] EWHC 1087 (Ch).

16–21   ADD REFERENCE TO NOTE 18A AT THE END OF THE PARAGRAPH.

ADD NEW NOTE 18A: See *SmithKline Beecham plc v Apotex Europe Ltd* [2006] EWCA Civ 658, at [25]–[31] *per* Jacob LJ.

16–23   NOTE 26: ADD: Where an interim injunction might affect the exercise of the right to freedom of expression, the position is slightly different. In such cases, it will normally be necessary to show more than a "real prospect" of success, but the court may dispense with this higher standard where particular circumstances make this necessary: *Cream Holdings Ltd v Banerjee* [2004] UKHL 44, at [20]–[23]; applied in *Boerhinger Ingelheim Ltd v Vetplus Ltd* [2007] EWCA Civ 583. See also *Douglas v Hello! Ltd* [2001] Q.B. 967 and *Imutran v Uncaged Campaigns Ltd* [2001] 2 All E.R. 385.

16–24   ADD TO MAIN TEXT AFTER REFERENCE TO NOTE 75: The test required by that section is less strict than the test which has traditionally been applied in defamation cases, and the old (stricter) test continues to apply [NOTE 75a] so that an interim injunction will be granted only in the clearest cases [NOTE 75b].

ADD NEW NOTE 75a: See *Greene v Associated Newspapers Ltd* [2004] EWCA Civ 1462.

ADD NEW NOTE 75b: *Bonnard v Perryman* [1891] 2 Ch 269.

16–25   DELETE THE FIRST SENTENCE AFTER AFTER THE HEADING "CLAIMANT'S UNDERTAK-ING", AND REPLACE WITH THE FOLLOWING: Interim injunctions are stop-gap remedies, which are granted on the basis of what is necessarily an incomplete picture. In deciding whether to grant such a remedy, the court will therefore wish to be satisfied in two respects: that an ultimately unsuccessful claimant can be obliged to compensate the defendant for having "wrongly" stopped his proposed activity, and that there is good reason to believe that the obligation will be honoured. The first of these is addressed by the giving of an "undertaking in damages" [81a]: a claimant is almost invariably required [82] to give such an undertaking; and an undertaking to this effect (unless expressly dis-avowed) will be implied if the court grants an injunction or accepts an undertaking in lie thereof [83].

DELETE THE SENTENCE WHICH FOLLOWS THE REFERENCE TO NOTE 84 AND REPLACE WITH THE FOLLOWING: Unless the court otherwise orders, an order for an injunction must contain an undertaking by the applicant to the court, to pay any damages which the respondent(s) (or any other "party" served with or notified of the order) sustain which the court considers the applicant should pay[84A]. The court will normally enforce such an undertaking to pay damages, if at the trial it appears that the injunction was wrongly granted[85], whether because the claimant is unable to prove at the trial the case he alleged at the granting of the injunction, or because the court granting the injunction took a wrong view of the law[86]. In relation to freezing orders, the practice is to require an undertaking whether the injunction is made before or after judgment[86a].

ADD NEW NOTE 81A: The grant of the injunction does not itself confer any right to compensation for loss or damage: *SmithKline Beecham plc v Apotex Europe Ltd* [2006] EWCA Civ 658. The need for a cross-undertaking is not absolute; but its existence is a "very material consideration" when considering whether an injunction should be granted: *SmithKline Beecham plc v Apotex Europe Ltd [2006] EWCA Civ 658*, at [26] (Jacob L.J.).

NOTE 82: INSERT AT BEGINNING OF NOTE: The requirement takes the form of refusing to grant injuncive relief unless a suitable cross-undertaking is given: see *SmithKline Beecham plc v Apotex Europe Ltd* [2006] EWCA Civ 658, at [24], [126] and [127], applying the dictum of Lord Diplock in *Hoffmann-La Roche & Co A.G. v Secretary of State for Trade and Industry* [1975] A.C. 295, 329 (H.L.), at 361; also *A-G v Albany Hotel Co* [1896] 2 Ch 696, at 699 *per* North J.

NOTE 83: DELETE, AND REPLACE WITH THE FOLLOWING: See *Tucker v New Brunswick Trading Co of London* (1890) 44 Ch.D. 249 (cross-undertaking implied upon grant of interim injunction, at least where the cross-undertaking is sought), and *Oberrheinische Metallwerke GmbH v Cocks* [1906] W.N. 127 (cross-undertaking to be implied where undertaking given to the court); see also [2006] L.M.C.L.Q. 181 (S. Gee Q.C.). A cross-undertaking given to the court is not retrospective, and will therefore only affect damages which are suffered by a person after (a) being joined as a party to the proceedings or (b) being served with (or notified of) the order: see *Smithkline Beecham plc and others v Apotex Europe Ltd and others* [2005] EWHC 1655 (Ch) at [41] and [49] (not challenged on appeal - see [2006] EWCA Civ 658 at [17] and [22].

NOTE 84: ADD: Where the court accepts a more limited form of undertaking (whether by mistake or otherwise) the position is different, and the order should stand as made: *Smithkline Beecham plc and others v Apotex Europe Ltd and others* [2005] EWHC 1655 (Ch) at [37] and [58]: but see [2006] LMCLQ 181 (S. Gee Q.C.) at pp.199–200.

INSERT NEW NOTE 84A: CPR 25PD, para. 5.1. The meaning of the word "party" is not clear, and it may be that (unless the court otherwise orders) the cross-undertaking will extend only to losses suffered by people who are parties to the proceedings: see *SmithKline Beecham plc v Apotex Europe Ltd* [2006] EWCA Civ 658 at [29]. This ambiguous term is repeated in the relevant practice forms (see PF39CH - Order for an Injunction (intended action), and PF40CH - Order for an Interim Injunction); but if the undertaking is actually given in those terms the ambiguity would probably be resolved by a strict (rather than a purposive) construction: see [2006] LMCLQ 181 (S Gee Q.C.), at 198–99, which also raises concerns in respect of the cross-undertaking to be implied under para.5.22 of the Chancery Guide and (at p.200–01) proposes a different (and more onerous) cross-undertaking. Save in respect of freezing orders, undertakings for the benefit of third parties have not routinely been granted, even after the practice direction came into effect in 1999: see eg *Miller Brewing Co v Mersey Docks & Harbour Co* [2003] EWHC 1606 (Ch), at [44]–[46] (criticised at [2006] LMCLQ 181 (S. Gee Q.C.) at pp.196–8); cf *Imutran Ltd v Uncaged Campaigns Ltd* [2002] F.S.R. 2. In March 2005, the standard form of interim injunction was amended so as to reflect C.P.R. 25PD 5.1: it may be that this will result in a change of practice.

INSERT NEW NOTE 86a: *Banco Nacional De Comercio Exterior S.N.C. v Empresa De Telecommunicaciones De Cuba S.A. (British Telecommunications plc intervening)*, at [41]. There may be exceptional cases where no undertaking is required (eg where the third party was not innocent): *ibid*, at [43].

NOTE 87: ADD: For a case where the amount payable was calculated by reference to the change in capital value of the defendant company, see *Johnson Control Systems Ltd v Techni-Track Europa Ltd (in administrative receivership)* [2003] EWCA Civ 1126.

NOTE 94: ADD: See also para.16.14.

16–26   ADD AT END: In an appropriate case, the court may also require the reconveyance of property, although it will not do this lightly on an interlocutory application [note 12a].

ADD NEW NOTE 12A: See *Esso Petroleum v Kingsowood Motors* [1974] Q.B. 142. at 157A-E.

16–28   NOTE 20: ADD: Although in the overwhelming majority of cases freezing orders are sought and obtained against the very defendants from whom the claimant seeks monetary compensation in the existing (or contemplated) proceedings, it is well established that such orders may also be made against persons in relation to whom the claimant asserts no cause of action and seeks no money judgment but in relation to whom there is an arguable case that assets held in their name (or under their control) are in truth beneficially owned by the defendant against whom the claim is made: see *H.M. Revenue & Customs v Egleton* [2006] EWHC 2313 (Ch) at [12], citing *TSB Private Bank International S.A. v Chabra* [1992] 1 W.L.R. 231. A freezing injunction may even be granted in some proceedings that do not directly involve a money claim, such as s.459 of the Companies Act 1985 (see *Re Premier Electronics (GB) Ltd* 2002] 2 B.C.L.C. 634), and winding-up proceedings (see *H.M. Revenue & Customs v Egleton* [2006] EWHC 2313 (Ch)); and, it would seem, the other circumstances suggested by the Australian High Court in *Cardile v LED Builders PTY Ltd* [1999] H.C.A. 18: see the *Egleton* case at [42] *per* Briggs J. However, an application for a freezing order made in the context of winding-up proceedings should, save in exceptional cases, be brought by a provisional liquidator and not by a petitioning (or supporting) creditor: *H.M. Revenue & Customs v Egleton* [2006] EWHC 2313 (Ch) at [48]–[51] *per* Briggs J.

NOTE 22: REPLACE with the following: Civil Jurisdiction and Judgments Act 1982, s.25(1) (as amended); *Republic of Haiti v Duvalier* [1990] 1 Q.B. 202; *X. v Y and another* [1990] 1 Q.B. 220. By the Civil Jurisdiction and Judgments Order (SI 2001/3929), s.25(1) of the 1982 Act now applies not only to states which are party to the Brussels and Lugano Conventions, but also to any country other than the U.K. which is a "Regulation State" (ie a member state of the E.U. other than Denmark). Arbitration claims are not "proceedings" for the purposes of s.25(1): see *ETI Euro Telecom N.V. v Republic of Bolivia* [2008] EWHC 1689 (COmm), at [22]–[25].

NOTE 38: ADD: One of those safeguards will usually be an undertaking, given by the party obtaining the order, not to seek to enforce it in another jurisdiction without the court's consent: *Dadourian Group International Inc v Simms* [2006] EWCA Civ 48 at [1]. **16–29**

NOTE 40: ADD: It is very unlikely that a worldwide (as opposed to a domestic) freezing order will be made in aid of a foreign judgment, unless the defendant is resident within the *U.K.: Banco Nacional De Commercio Exterior S.N.C. v Empressa De Telecommunicaciones De Cuba S.A. (British Telecommunications plc intervening)* [2007] EWCA Civ 662 at [27]–[30].

NOTE 46: ADD: Commonly, cross-claims will be netted-off, unless set-off is not permissible under the relevant system of law: see *Fourie v Le Roux* [2005] EWCA Civ 204, at [65] (not challenged on appeal). **16–30**

ADD TO MAIN TEXT AFTER REFERENCE TO NOTE 57: Where the assets are held at the defendant's bank, the bank does not owe any duty of care to the claimant simply by reason of the making of the freezing order. If assets are dissipated, the claimant's loss is pure economic loss and (applying established principles) a bank could only be liable for such loss if it had voluntarily assumed responsibility for the non-dissipation of the defendant's assets: but the obligation not to dispose of the defendant's assets is imposed by court order rather than by voluntary act of the bank. [NOTE 57a]. Worldwide freezing orders are usually given on condition that the person obtaining the order undertakes not to enforce the order abroad without the court's permission [NOTE 57b], and the Court of Appeal has recently laid down 8 guidelines which are to be applied when considering whether permission should be given [NOTE 57c]. **16–31**

NOTE 56: ADD: See also [2006] L.M.C.L.Q. 181 (S. Gee QC) at 186–91.

ADD NEW NOTE 57a: *Commissioners of Customs & Excise v Barclays Bank plc* [2006] UKHL 28, reversing [2004] EWCA Civ 1555. See also [2005] C.L.J. 26 (O'Sullivan).

ADD NEW NOTE 57b: *Dadourian Group International Inc v Simms* [2006] EWCA Civ 48, at [1].

ADD NEW NOTE 57c: See *Dadourian Group International Inc v Simms* [2006] EWCA Civ 48, at [26]–[49]. The 8 guidelines are as follows: (1) The principle applying to the grant of permission to enforce a WFO abroad is that the grant of that permission should be just and convenient for the purpose of ensuring the effectiveness of the WFO, and that it is not oppressive to the parties to the English proceedings or to third parties who may be joined in the foreign proceedings. (2) All the relevant circumstances and options need to be considered. In particular consideration should be given to granting relief on terms, eg terms as to the extension to third parties of the undertaking to compensate for costs incurred as a result of the WFO and as to the type of proceedings that may be commenced abroad. Consideration should also be given to the proportionality of the steps proposed to be taken abroad, as well as the form of any order. (3)The interests of the applicant should be balanced against the interests of the other parties to the proceedings and any new party likely to be joined to the foreign proceedings. (4) Permission should not normally be given in terms that would enable the applicant to obtain relief in the foreign proceedings shich is superior to the relief given by the WFO. (5) The evidence in support of the application for permission should contain all the information (so far as it can reasonably be obtained in the time available) necessary to enable the Judge to reach an informed decision, including evidence as to the applicable law and practice in the foreign court, evidence as to the nature of the proposed proceedings to be commenced and evidence as to teh assets believed to be located in the jurisdiction of the foreign court and the names of the parties by whom such assets are held. (6) The standard of proof as to the existence of assets that are both within the WFO and within the jurisdiction of the foreign court is a real prospect, ie the applicant must show that there is a real prospect that such assets are located within the jurisdiction of the foreign court in question. (7) There must be evidence of a risk of dissipation of the assets in question. (8) Normally the application should be made on notice to the respondent; but in cases of urgency, where it is just to do so, permission may be given without notice to the party against whom relief will be sought in the foreign proceedings - but in such cases the party should have the earliest practicable opportunity of having the matter reconsidered by the court at a hearing of which he is given notice.

16–32   NOTE 60: ADD: The court may, by requiring suitable undertakings, impose limits on the use that may be made of the answers given in such cross-examination; for the circumstances in which it may be appropriate for a court to permit use in subsequent committal proceedings, see *Dadourian Group International Inc v Simms (No.2)* [2006] EWCA Civ 1745, at [20]–[25].

16–35   ADD NEW NOTE NOTE 95A AFTER "The Principles upon which relief is now granted may be summarised as follows".

NOTE 91: ADD: An English court may not restrain the commencement or continuation of proceedings in another state which is party to the

Brussels Convention on Jurisdiction and the Enforcement of Judgments in Civil and Commercial Matters 1968, other than in the exceptional cases listed at Art.28 of that convention: see *Turner v Grovitt* [2005] 1 A.C. 101 (ECJ); also [2004] L.Q.R. 529 (Briggs). The barriers to the granting of an anti-suit injunction do not operate for matters outside the scope of the Brussels Convention however, so that an English court may grant anti-suit injunctive relief in support of an arbitration pending in England and Wales: see *Through Transport Mutual Insurance Association (Eurasia) Ltd v New India Assurance Co Ltd* [2004] EWCA Civ 1598.

ADD NEW NOTE 95a: These principles address both the existence of the court's jurisdiction to grant interim relief, and the settled principles that apply where that jurisdiction is being invoked: see *Albon (t/a NA Carriage Co) v Naza Motor Trading Sdn Bhd* [2007] EWCA Civ 1124, at [7].For a different formulation of the principles, see *Glencore International AG v Exeter Shipping Ltd* [2002] EWCA Civ 528, at [42]–[43]. For an application of these principles, see *Sabah Shipyard (Pakistan) Ltd v The Islamic Republic of Pakistan* [2002] EWCA Civ 1643, at [41] and [45] per Waller LJ; also *Albon (t/a NA Carriage Co) v Naza Motor Trading* (above).

NOTE 99: ADD: See also *OT Africa Line Ltd v Magic Sportswear Corporation Ltd and others* [2005] EWCA Civ 710.

DELETE THE PARAGRAPH, AND REPLACE AS FOLLOWS: (b) *Arbitrations*. If **16–36** parties have expressly agreed that their disputes should be resolved under arbitration, then the effect of the Arbitration Act 1996 is to identify and limit the court's role. Part of the court's role is to support the arbitral process: by staying court proceedings which fall within the scope of the agreement, [NOTE 1] and by making interim orders in relation to evidence (eg its preservation or inspection), the sale of property, the granting of injunctions or the appointment of a receiver [NOTE 1a]. Another part (where the seat of the arbitration is within England and Wales or Northern Ireland) is to supervise the arbitral process: whether by adjudicating on questions of jurisdiction [NOTE 2] or considering challenges to any award made [NOTE 2a]. The provisions of the Arbitration Act 1996 do not oust the court's jurisdiction (under s.37 of the Supreme Court Act 1981) to grant an injunction restraining the conduct of an arbitration [NOTE 3]; but they provide a powerful reason why that jurisdiction should be exercised only sparingly. With the above in mind, the position would seem to be as follows. In relation to foreign arbitrations (ie those whose seat is elsewhere than England Wales or Northern Ireland), the court may restrain the arbitration if two conditions are satisfied: (i) the arbitration must be vexatious or oppressive, or have been brought in breach of contract [NOTE 3a]; and (ii) the case must be regarded as sufficiently exceptional to justify a departure from the principles of the law of international arbitration agreed under the New York Convention and recognised by the Arbitration Act 1996 [NOTE 3b]. In relation to domestic arbitrations, the restraint of arbitral proceedings may also be justified in circumstances which mirror those in which the existence of an arbitration agreement would not require a stay under the 1986 Act [NOTE 4]: ie, where the arbitration agreement is null and void [NOTE 4a]; if it is inoperative, or if it is incapable of being performed. An injunction to restrain further proceedings in an arbitration will not be granted simply because a party has been guilty of inordinate or inexcuable delay [NOTE 4b]. Nor will an injunction normally be granted where the complaint is that the arbitrator is biased: in such a case, the appropriate remedy is to seek the arbitrator's removal [NOTE 5].

NOTE 1: Arbitration Act 1996, s.9. The confidential nature of arbitration proceedings is such, once proceedings have been stayed under s.9, a stranger to the arbitration should not normally be permitted access to documents on the court's file: *Glidepath BV v Thompson* [2005] EWHC 818 (Comm). Section 9 applies wherever the seat of the arbitration might be: see s.2(1) and s.2(2)

NOTE 1a: Arbitration Act 1996, s.44; *Hiscox Underwriting Ltd v Dickson Mancester & Co Ltd* [2004] EWHC 479 (Comm). Section 44 applies wherever the seat of the arbitration might be: see s.2(1) and s.2(2).

NOTE 2: Arbitration Act 1996, s.32 and s.72. Challenges to an award on the basis of substantive jurisdiction are governed by s.67.

NOTE 2a: Arbitration Act 1996, ss.67–71.

NOTE 3: *Weissfisch v Julius* [2006] EWCA Civ 218; *Elektrim S.A. v Vivendi Universal S.A. and others* [2007] EWHC 571 (Comm); *J Jarvis & Sons Ltd v Blue Circle Dartford Estates Ltd* [2007] EWHC 1262 (TCC), at [40].

NOTE 3a: This is the test for "anti-suit" injunctions: see *Intermet FZCO v Ansol Ltd* [2007] EWHC 226 (Comm); also para.16–35 above. However, that test is not sufficient in cases where the proceedings sought to be restrained are arbitral: *Elektrim SA v Vivendi Universal SA* [2007] EWHC 571 (Comm), at [77].

NOTE 3b: *Weissfisch v Julius* [2006] EWCA Civ 218, at [33]; *J Jarvis & Sons Ltd v Blue Circle Dartford Estates Ltd* [2007] EWHC 1262 (TCC), at [40].

NOTE 4: Arbitration Act 1996, s.9(4).

NOTE 4a: See also *Kitts v Moore* [1895] 1 Q.B. 253. For an example of an arbitration stayed on the grounds that the arbitration agreement was (at least arguably) a forgery, see *Albon (t/a NA Carriage Co) v Naza Motor Trading Sdn Bhd* [2007] EWCA Civ 1124.

NOTE 4b: *Bremer Vulkan Schiffbau und Maschinenfabrik v South India Shipping Corp Ltd* [1981] A.C. 909.

NOTE 5: See *Weissfisch v Julius* (above), at [32] where the following points are made: (i) it is not uncommon for arbitrators to be called on to consider submissions that they are not competent to act by reason of bias; (ii) in such circumstances the arbitrator's decision will not be final, provided that the seat of the arbitration is in a country where the courts exercise an appropriate supervisory jurisdiction, and (iii) where the arbitrator's consideration of such submissions is only a first step in determining the quesiton of bias, there is nothing untoward in the arbitrator's considering the question. Under the Arbitration Act 1996, questions of bias are regulated by s.24: an application to remove the arbitrator may be made; but the arbitration is to remain on foot until the application has been disposed of. If questions of bias arise in an arbitration whose seat is in a country where there is no (or no "appropriate") supervisory jurisdiction, that fact may amount to an exceptional circumstance justifying an English court's intervention.

NOTE 10: ADD: Where the injunction restrains an unlawful use of land, **16–37** it is wrong in principle to suspend its effect until such time as the use becomes lawful; rather, it should be suspended for so long as may be reasonable for the unlawful use to cease: *Mid-Bedfordshire D.C. v Brown* [2004] EWCA Civ 1709.

CHAPTER 17

RECEIVERS

NOTE 2: ADD: See also *Capewell v Revenue and Customs Commissioners* **17–1**
[2007] UKHL 2, at [19].

DELETE THE FIRST SETENCE AND REPLACE WITH THE FOLLOWING: The court may **17–3**
appoint a receiver at any stage [7a]: before proceedings have started; in
existing proceedings or on or after judgment. There are two purposes
for making such an appointment.

ADD AT END OF PARAGRAPH: A receiver appointed by the court must be
an individual[9a].

INSERT NEW NOTE 7A: C.P.R. 69.2(1).

INSERT NEW NOTE 9A: C.P.R. 69.1(2).

NOTE 6: DELETE NOTE AND ADD: See below, para.38–55. **17–5**

DELETE FIRST SENTENCE OF SECTION (2), AND REPLACE WITH THE FOLLOWING: (2) **17–7**
AUTHORITY . Historically, a receiver was always required to provide
security for his duty to account; and the receiver had no authority until
security had been given [37]. It remains the case that acceptable security
will normally have to be provided, but a receiver now has authority
from the moment that he is appointed. The form of the security, and the
date by which it is to be supplied, will normally be specified at the time
when the court makes the order appointing the receiver [37a]. Where the
receiver is a licensed insolvency practitioner, it is possible that acceptable security is already in place: in such a case, the court will merely
need to satisfy itself that the receiver's existing bond (provided under
the Insolvency Practitioner Regulations 1990) provides acceptable cover:
ie, that it guarantees a suitable sum, and that the cover provided by the
bond extends to appointment as a court-appointed receiver [37b]. In
other cases, security will normally have to take the form of a guarantee
provided by a clearing bank or insurance company [37c]. Although the
court may direct that the receiver should not begin to act until security
has been provided [37d], the "default setting" is that the receiver is
entitled to act as soon as the order making the appointment is made. If
the receiver fails to provide security (or to provide evidence that a
satisfactory bond is in place) by the due date, the court may terminate
the appointment and the receiver's authority comes to an end [37e].

ADD NEW NOTE 37A: See C.P.R. 69PD, para. 7.1.

ADD NEW NOTE 37B: See C.P.R. 69PD, paras. 7.1(2), 7.2(1) and 7.3(1).

ADD NEW NOTE 37C: See C.P.R. 69PD, paras. 7.1(1), 7.2(2) and 7.3(2). The court's approval is required in respect of the identity of the bank (or insurance company) as well as the form of the guarantee: *ibid*, para.7.3(2).

ADD NEW NOTE 37D: See C.P.R. 69.5(1).

ADD NEW NOTE 37E: See C.P.R. 69.5(2).

17–9   DELETE PARAGRAPH, AND REPLACE WITH THE FOLLOWING: (b) *Appointed by the court.* A receiver may only charge for his services if the court so directs [49]. The court may also specify who is to be responsible for paying the receiver, and any fund or property from which the receiver may recover his remuneration [50]. If the receiver is to be entitled to receive remuneration, the basis for identifying that remuneration must be identified by the court [50a]. It would seem that the court is able to identify any suitable basis for remuneration [50b]. In some cases, the court may authorise remuneration by reference to factors which are wholly objective [50c]: e.g., by reference to time actually spent (the court identifying the rate at whic time may be charged) or by reference to the amount of income received (the court identifying the rate at which commission on that amount may be charged) [50d]. However, in many cases the court is likely to direct that the amount of the receiver's remuneration will be such sum as is subsequently determined by the court [50e]; and, if it does so, it may also identify the basis upon which the court is to reach that determination [50f]. If a receiver incurs expenses in the course of the receivership, then these are not regarded as part of his remuneration: rather, they are accounted for as part of the receiver's account for the assets he has recovered [50g].

NOTE 49: DELETE EXISTING NOTE, AND REPLACE WITH THE FOLLOWING: See C.P.R. 69.7(1). The wording of C.P.R. 69.7(1)(b) suggests that the court's direction must be prospective: ie, the court's power is limited to directing that costs be paid in respect of the receiver's future services.

NOTE 50: DELETE EXISTING NOTE AND REPLACE WITH THE FOLLOWING: See C.P.R. 69.7(2). The terms of C.P.R. 69.7 should be read with caution. Before the Civil Procedure Rules, a receiver was (and was merely) entitled to be indemnified (in respect of costs and expenses) out of the assets which were the subject-matter of the receivership: see *Boehm v Goodall* [1911] 1 Ch 155, at 161 (per Warrington J) and *Mellor v Mellor* [1992] 1 W.L.R. 517; also *Evans v Clayhope Properties Ltd* [1988] 1 W.L.R. 358. C.P.R. 69.7 sets out a procedural code, but (i) does not (and cannot) make any fundamental change in the general law of receivership and (ii) bearing in mind the heavy responsibilities which a receiver accepts on his/her appointment, cannot effect a retrospective change in the terms of that appointment: *Capewell v Revenue and Customs Commissioners* [2007] UKHL 2, at [26]–[27].

ADD NEW NOTE 50A: See C.P.R. 69.7(1)(b).

ADD NEW NOTE 50B: C.P.R. 69.7(3) expressly contemplates that the court may direct that the amount of the receiver's remuneration may be identified in some other way than by a determination of the court.

ADD NEW NOTE 50C: The court will normally detemine the amount of the receiver's remunderation on the basis of the criteria in C.P.R. 69.7(4): see C.P.R. 69PD, para.9.2, and note 50f below. With this in mind, a receiver's costs are only likely to be determined on an objective basis in relatively simple cases.

ADD NEW NOTE 50D: Remuneration at five per cent on the amount of income received has (historically) been regarded as usual for straightforward cases: see *Day v Croft* (1840) 2 Beav. 488.

ADD NEW NOTE 50E: See C.P.R. 69.7(3). The court may direct that such a determination be carried out by a costs judge: C.P.R. 69.7(5). Where a direction is made under C.P.R. 69.7(3), the receiver is not entitled to recover any remuneration for his services unless and until a determination is made: C.P.R. 69.7(3)(a). An application for such a determination may be made "at any time", and it follows that a receiver may seek a determination (for work done to date) part-way through the receivership.

ADD NEW NOTE 50F: Unless the court orders otherwise, the remuneration determined pursuant to a direction under C.P.R. 69.7(3) should be reasonable and proportionate in all the circumstances, and should take into account the matters identified at C.P.R. 69.7(4): (a) the time properly given by the receiver and his staff to the receivership; (b) the complexity of the receivership; (c) the effectiveness with which the receiver appears to be carrying out (or to have carried out) his duties, and (d) the value and nature of the subject-matter of the receivership.

ADD NEW NOTE 50G: See C.P.R. 69PD, para.9.6. It would seem to be the receiver who bears the risk that outgoings may exceed total income: cp *Evans v Clayhope Properties Ltd, supra*.

ADD AT THE END OF THE PARAGRAPH: The position may be different if the **17–20** building comprises (or includes) leasehold flats since, since those may be premises to which Part II of the Landlord and Tenant Act 1987 applies[2a]: that statute provides a separate code for the appointment of a "manager"[2b], which is outside the scope of this text.

ADD NEW NOTE 2A: The general rule is that Part II of the 1987 Act will apply to premises (whether they comprise the whole or only a part of a building), if the building or part contains two or more flats: Landlord and Tenant Act 1987, s.21(2). There are exceptions to that general rule, in the case of certain types of landlord and in the case of certain types of land: see Landlord and Tenant Act 1987, s.21(3). By s.21(3)(a), Part II does not apply where the landlord is (i) an "exempt landlord" as that term is defined at s.58(1), or (ii) a "resident landlord" as that term is defined at s.58(2), as modified by s.21(3A) of the 1987 Act. By s.21(3)(b),

Part II of the 1987 Act does not apply to premises which are included within the functional land of any charity.

ADD NEW NOTE 2B: See Landlord and Tenant Act 1987, ss.21–24. A manager under the Act is appointed by a leasehold valuation tribunal, and is to exercise such functions (whether management functions or the functions of a receiver) as the tribunal thinks fit: s.24(1).

17–24   ADD NEW PARAGRAPH TO THE END OF THE TEXT: The insolvency Act 1986 makes specific provision for the appointment of managers and receivers is certain cases of personal insolvency. Save in cases where the bankrupt's estate vests in a trutee immediately on the making of the bankruptcy order [note 27a], the effect of the bankruptcy order is to appoint the Official Receiver as receiver of the bankrupt's estate for the period up to the point where the estate vests in the trustee in bankruptcy [note 27b]. During the period of his appointment, the Official Receiver's function is to protect the estate: to this end, he has the same powers as if he were a receiver or manager appointed by the High Court, and is entitled to sell (or otherwise dispose of) goods which are perishable or whose value is likely to diminish unless disposed of [note 27c]. The Official Receiver may also be appointed as an interim receiver, at any point between the presentation of a bankruptcy petition and the making of a bankruptcy order [note 27d]. The court's power to make such an order only arises where it is satisfied that the appointment of an interim receiver is necessary for the protection of the debtor's property [note 27e]. Unless the order appointing the Official Receiver provides otherwise, his rights, powers, duties and immunities as interim receiver are the same as they would be if the receivership arose under section 287 of the 1986 Act [note 27f]. Although the court has a specific power to appoint the Official Receiver as interim receiver of the debtor's property, that does not exclude its general power to appoint some other person as interim receiver under section 37 of the Supreme Court Act 1981 [note 27g]; but it is to be doubted whether it could exercise both jurisdictions so as to appoint two different people to act as receiver at the same time [note 27h]. Whether the appointment arises under section 286 or section 287, the Official Receiver's role as manager (as opposed to his role as receiver) is subject to section 370 of the Insolvency Act 1986 [note 27i].

Footnotes:

ADD NOTE 27a: Insolvency Act 1986, s.287(5).

ADD NOTE 27b: Insolvency Act 1986, s.287(1).

ADD NOTE 27c: Insolvency Act 1986, s.287(2).

ADD NOTE 27d: Insolvency Act 1986, s.286.

ADD NOTE 27e: Insolvency Act 1986, s.286(1)&(2).

ADD NOTE 27f: Insolvency Act 1986, s.287(3).

ADD NOTE 27g: *Rio Properties Inc. v Gibson Dunn & Crutcher and another* [2004] EWCA Civ 1043. It is only exceptional circumstances which would justify the exercise of the court's general power under SCA 1981 s.37 rather than IA 1986 s.286: *ibid.*

ADD NOTE 27H: While not deciding this point, the Court of Appeal has indicated that it would take the most exceptional circumstances to justify the making of such an order: *Rio Properties v Gibson Dunn & Crutcher*, at [54], [56].

ADD NOTE 27I: Insolvency Act 1986, s.287(1).

Chapter 18

PERSONAL MONETARY CLAIMS

ADD REFERENCE TO NEW NOTE 5A, AFTER THE WORD "TRUSTEE" IN THE SECOND **18-4** SENTENCE.

ADD NOTE 5A: Accounts by fiduciaries are considered at para.7–127 ff.

NOTE 6. DELETE THE SEMI-COLON AND THE TEXT WHICH FOLLOWS IT.

NOTE 43: ADD: The need to rely upon principles first introduced into **18-11** the law in 1858 (before the administration of law and equity was fused) may be ripe for re-examination: see *Harris v Williams-Wynne* [2006] EWA Civ 104, at [54] *per* Chadwick L.J. However, it is suggested that those principles remain relevant in the modern age - at least when considering the compensation to be made in respect of future (as opposed to historic) wrongs: see proposition (3) in the main text.

NOTE 55: DELETE THE NOTE, AND REPLACE WITH THE FOLLOWING: *Sayers v Collyer* (1884) 24 Ch.D. 103; also Landau v Curton [1962] E.G.D. 369, at 375 (Cross J). But see note 57 below, and the cases there cited.

NOTE 57: DELETE SECOND SENTENCE OF NOTE, AND REPLACE WITH THE FOLLOW-ING: In some cases acquiesence will be a ground inducing the court to award damages in lieu of equitable relief; but in others, it may be an entire bar to all relief: *Sayers v Collyer* (1884) 24 Ch.D. 103, at 110 (per Fry LJ). It is likely that acquiescence is a form of estoppel, the critical question being whether (by reason of the claimant's words or conduct) it is unconscionable for the claim to be brought in a particular way, or for it to be brought at all: see *De Bussche v Alt* (1878) 8 Ch.D. 286, 307 (C.A.), at 314; *Shaw v Applegate* [1877] 1 W.L.R. 970, at 978 (Buckley LJ) and 780 (Goff LJ); also *Gafford v Graham* [1999] 3 E.G.L.R. 75 at 78–9; cf *Goldsworthy v Brickell* [1987] Ch 378, at 410. See also para.16–16.

NOTE 62: ADD: The position is no different if the right being asserted is a right to light, provided that there has been (or will be) an actionable interference with that right: see *Regan v Paul Properties DFP No.1 Ltd* [2006] EWCA Civ 1319. Where the grant of an injunction would be oppressive to the defendant, and its refusal would only cause the claimant minor loss (which may be sufficiently compensated), then damages in lieu of injunctive relief should be ordered: *Small v Oliver & Saunders Developments Ltd* [2006] EWHC 1293 (Ch), applying *Shelfer v City of London Electric Lighting Company* [1895] 1 Ch 287, at pp 322–323 *per* A.L. Smith L.J.

NOTE 77: ADD: The exercise required by the section is essentially a balancing exercise, in order to determine what would be "equitable" in the circumstances. With this in mind there is no magic to be attached to the word "loss", which includes financial loss and what might loosely be described as "detriment": *UCB Corporate Services Ltd v Thomason and another* [2005] EWCA Civ 225.

18–12   NOTE 82: ADD: See also [2003] R.L.R. 101 (Edelman). It follows that the juridical bases for directing an account of profits and for awarding damages on the *Wrotham Park* basis are "highly similar": see *WWF -World Wide Fund for Nature v World Wrestling Federation Entertainment Inc* [2007] EWCA Civ 286, at [59]–[60]

18–15   NOTE 91. ADD: Where a fiduciary receives a profit in breach of fiduciary duty, that profit is properly to be regarded as part of the trust assets for which account should be given: see para.7–127 ff.

18–18   AT THE END OF PRINCIPLE (1), INSERT REFERENCE TO NEW NOTE 97A.

NOTE 97: ADD: See also *WWF - World Wide Fund for Nature v World Wrestling Federation Entertainment Inc* [2006] EWHC 184 (Ch) at [174] per Peter Smith J, where the basic approach taken by the Judge in *Amec* was adopted. The principles applied by Peter Smith J have been approved by the Court of Appeal, subject to the caveat that there are no absolute rules: *Lunn Poly v Liverpool & Lancashire Properties Ltd* [2006] EWCA Civ 430 at [23] and [24]. The decision in the *WWF* case was reversed on appeal, on the basis that (on the facts of that case) the claiming of *Wrotham Park* damages amounted to an abuse of process: see [2007] EWCA Civ 286.

NEW NOTE 97A: As the expression "normally" suggests, there will be cases where it is appropriate to use a different valuation date: *Lunn Poly v Liverpool & Lancashire Properties Ltd* [2006] EWCA Civ 430, at [17]–[18] *per* Neuberger L.J.

18–30   ADD A REFERENCE TO A NEW NOTE [40A] AT THE END OF SUB-PARAGRAPH (1).

ADD NEW NOTE 40A: In cases of co-ownership, the purpose for which the property is held will normally be to enable the co-owners to live together. In general, payment of outgoings or improvements prior to the date of separation will be in accordance with the arrangements between the parties and the common purpose of the trust. The relevant period for the purposes of equitable accounting will ordinarily start on the date of separation, because that is normally an event which supersedes (or amounts to a breach or failure to honour) the earlier arrangements: *Clarke v Harlowe* [2005] EWHC B20 (Ch), at [39]. The position is similar in respect of an occupation rent - while the purpose of the trust continues (eg to provide a home for the children of one or both co-owners), no occupation rent will ordinarily be payable: *Stack v Bowden* [2005] EWCA Civ 857 (see also note 48 below).

NOTE 48: ADD: See also *Stack v Dowden* [2005] EWCA Civ 857, where no order for an occupation rent was made in favour of the absentee because

(i) the purposes for which the property was held included the provision of a home not only for the claimant and the defendant, but also for their children; (ii) the claimant had previously given an undertaking not to live in the property; (iii) until sale, the property was needed as the children's home, and (iv) there was no suggestion that the defendant was in any way responsible for any delays in achieving that sale. *Stack v Dowden* is noted at [2005] Conv. 555 (Cooke).

ADD TO FOOTNOTE 51. The regime set out in ss. 12–13 of the Trusts of Land and Appointment of Trustees Act 1996 is not exhaustive, and the pre-existing principles of equitable accounting continues to apply: *French v Barcham* [2008] W.T.L.R. 1813.

CHAPTER 19

DEFINITION AND CLASSIFICATION OF TRUSTS

This definition of a trust was applied in *Clarence House Ltd v National* **19–2**
Westminster Bank plc [2009] EWHC 77 (Ch), [2009] 3 All E.R. 175 (Ch).

REPLACE SECOND PARAGRAPH WITH THE FOLLOWING: Indeed, to ask who is **19–3**
the "real owner" may oversimplify the relationship: the question
presupposes a universally applicable conception of ownership and a
single conception of a trust. It is better to approach the question in
functional terms. In reality, the incidents of ownership are split between
the trustee and the beneficiary according to the terms of the particular
trust. The nature and extent of their entitlements cannot be determined
in the abstract without referring to the terms of the trust instrument
[*CPT Custodian Pty. Ltd. v Commissioner of State Revenue* [2005] HCA 53,
(2005) 79 A.L.J.R. 1724]. The relevant conception of ownership may also
depend on the context in which the question is asked. In determining,
for example, whether an express trustee is the real owner of property, it
may be more productive to ask whether, and to whom, he is accountable for his management of the property, and whether he owes a
fundamental duty not to act dishonestly [D.J. Hayton, Ch. 3 in A.J.
Oakley (ed.), *Trends in Contemporary Trust Law* (1996); *Armitage v Nurse*
[1998] Ch. 241]. If he does, it can be said, at least negatively, that the
trustee is not the "real" owner of the property [Purpose trusts illustrate
the possibility that a trustee may hold property without any other
person having beneficial rights to it. The suspension of beneficial
ownership may be the very reason why the settlor created the trust: D.J.
Hayton (2001) 117 L.Q.R. 96; and P. Matthews, Ch. 1 in A.J. Oakley (ed.),
Trends in Contemporary Trust Law (1996)]. The terms of tax legislation,
rather than any abstract conception of ownership, may determine
whether a beneficiary is to be treated as having a sufficient interest in
the trust to be liable to tax [*Gartside v Inland Revenue Commissioners*
[1968] A.C. 553, 617–618 *per* Lord Wilberforce; *CPT Custodian Pty. Ltd. v
Commissioner of State Revenue* [2005] HCA 53, (2005) 79 A.L.J.R. 1724].
Similarly, the terms of company or insolvency legislation may require a
court to inquire whether a trustee or beneficiary is entitled to exercise
the voting rights or voting power attaching to shares held on trust. To
ask who is the "real owner" of the shares would be simplistic [*E.g., Re
Kilnoore Ltd. (in liquidation)* [2005] EWHC 1410 (Ch), [2005] 3 All E.R.
730].

19–5   ADD TO SENTENCE FOLLOWING ING NOTE 32: The doctrine is a general one. It would also apply to prevent the enforcement of an express trust or a constructive trust arising out of an informal agreement: *Barrett v Barrett* [2008] EWHC 1061 (Ch), [2008] B.P.I.R. 817.

19–11   ADD TO NOTE 52: See generally P. Matthews [2005] P.C.B. 266, 335.

ADD TO NOTE 54: This passage was considered in *Nelson v Greening & Sykes (Builders) Ltd* [2007] EWCA Civ 1358, [2008] 8 E.G. 158. There it was held that the authorities do not establish that an intermediate trustee ceases to be a trustee as a matter of law, but only that, in the case of a trust and sub-trust of personal property, the trustees may decide, as a matter of practicality, that it is more convenient to deal directly with the beneficiary of the sub-trust.

19–13   NOTE 59. AFTER *"Re Denley's Trust Deed* [1969] 1 Ch 373"

ADD: (distinguished in *Ernst & Young v Central Guaranty Trust Company (No. 2)* (2004) 7 1 T.E.L.R. 69 (Alberta). And see also *Hiranand v Harilela* (2004) 7 I.T.E.L.R 450 (Hong Kong).

19–28   ADD AT END OF FOOTNOTE 7: In the case of a dishonest assistance claim the normal primary limitation period is six years from the date of accrual of the cause of action, though this may be postponed by reason of the operation of s.21(3) and s.32 of the Limitation Act 1980.

CHAPTER 20

EXPRESS PRIVATE TRUSTS

FOOTNOTE 67: ADD: For a situation which was more consistent with that of **20–22**
a banker and customer, rather than that of a trustee and beneficiary, see
Azam v Iqbal [2008] Bus L R 168.

NOTE 93. ADD: For a further article see [2008] C.L.J. 176 (Conaglen). **20–48**

NOTE 94. AT THE END ADD: applied in *Minwalla v Minwalla* (2005) 7
I.T.E.L.R. 457. *Hitch v Stone* and subsequent authorities were considered
in *Re Nurkowski* [2005] BPIR 842.

CHAPTER 21

EXPRESS PUBLIC (OR CHARITABLE) TRUSTS

ADD TO NOTE 1: Picarda, *The Law and Practice Relating to Charities* (4th ed.). **21–1**

NOTE 64. ADD: In New Zealand it has been held that the provision of **21–11** superannuation style benefits by church-based funds established for the dominant purpose of providing benefits for ministers of religion and their families was a charitable purpose: *Hester v Commissioner of Inland Revenue* (2005) 7 I.T.E.L.R.420.

ADD TO PARAGRAPH: Scientology has been held not to be a religion for the purposes of charity law since its practices lack the reverence and veneration of a supreme being which are necessary to constitute worship in charity law: *Re Church of Scientology* (1999) [2005] W.T.L.R. 1151.

ADD TO FOOTNOTE 85: *Hanchett-Stamford v Attorney General* [2008] **21–12** EWHC 330 (Ch), [2009] Ch. 173.

ADD TO TEXT FOLLOWING FOOTNOTE 87: In this context, politicial purposes are predominantly those that involve a change in the law or in government policy.

ADD TO NOTE 44: For an application of s.34, see *Re Harding* (decd.)[2007] **21–16** EWHC 3 (Ch), [2008] 1 Ch. 235.

NOTE 78. ADD: *Ulrich v Treasury Solicitor* [2005] 1 All E.R., [2005] **21–23** W.T.L.R. 385, [2005] 7 I.T.E.L.R. 552.

NOTE 75. ADD: This passage was cited in *Re Estate of Bruce (decd)* (2004) **21–36** 7 I.T.E.L.R. 280 (Prince Edward island)).

NOTE 38. ADD: *Re Snowden was considered in A-G v Trustees of the British* **21–43** *Museum* [2005] EWHC 1089 (Ch), [2005] 3 W.L.R. 396.

NOTES 50 AND 51. As for when a reverter takes place under the **21–44** Reverter of Sites Act 1841 see *Frazer v Canterbury Diocesan Board of Finance (No. 2)* [2005] 3 W.L.R. 964, HL.

NOTE 80. ADD: See *Mersey Docks and Harbour Board Trustees v Gibb* **21–51** [1861–1873] All E.R. Rep. 397 (HL), and *Re The Christian Brothers of Ireland in Ireland* [2004] W.T.L.R. 1079 (Canada). There is no doctrine of charitable immunity under which, for example, charitable trust funds canot be used to compensate tort claimants against a charity.

CHAPTER 22

TRUSTS ARISING TO ENFORCE AN INFORMALLY EXPRESSED INTENTION

INSERT AFTER FIRST SENTENCE OF PARAGRAPH: In general, the vendor's duty as **22–3** trustee is to preserve the property until completion in its state as at the time of the contract: *Englewood Properties Ltd. v Patel* [2005] EWHC 188 (Ch), [2005] 1 W.L.R. 1961.

INSERT AT END OF FIRST PARAGRAPH: Equally, he would not generally be liable for failing to take steps in relation to other land which might indirectly affect the property under the contract: *Englewood Properties Ltd. v Patel* [2005] EWHC 188 (Ch), [2005] 1 W.L.R. 1961 (failure to include restrictive covenants in conveyances of neighbouring land).

ADD AFTER SECOND PARAGRAPH: The interest of the purchaser is not **22–4** absolute and the beneficial entitlement to the property may be best treated as passing to him by stages as the various conditions upon which completion of the contract depends are fulfilled. The purchaser's right may determine, for example, if one of the parties rescinds the contract or if the vendor fails to make good title: *Jerome v Kelly* [2004] W.T.L.R. 681. This shows the extent to which the incidents of the trust relationship express and depend upon the underlying contract between the parties.

REPLACE FOOTNOTE 47 WITH THE FOLLOWING: (1874) L.R. 18 Eq. 315. See **22–12** *Kodilinye [1982] Conv. 14 and Jaconelli [2006] Conv. 432.*

ADD FOONOTE AFTER FINAL SENTENCE OF PARAGRAPH: This sentence was **22–31** cited with approval in *Olins v Walters* [2009] EWCA 782, [2009] Ch. 212 at [40].

AMEND TO OPENING SENTENCE OF FIRST PARAGRAPH: The agreement must **22–32** amount to a contract at law. But it is unnecessary for all terms to be defined so precisely that they could be enforced by an order for specific performance. It is enough that the intentions of T1 and T2 to create the agreement are sufficiently clear for their conscience to be bound in equity: *Olins v Walters* [2009] EWCA 782, [2009] Ch. 212 at [36]–[41] per Mummery L.J.

REPLACE SECOND SENTENCE WITH THE FOLLOWING: Until the first death, **22–33** either may withdraw from the arrangement by giving notice to the other party, and no trust interest arises for the intended beneficiary of the agreement: *Stone v Hoskins* [1905] P. 194; *Barns v Barns* [2003] HCA 9, (2003) 214 C.L.R. 169 at [85]. *Cf.* T.G. Youdan (1979) 24 U.Tor.L.J. 390 at 406–410.

REPLACE THIRD SENTENCE WITH THE FOLLOWING: Any material alteration by one party of his will will prevent the arrangement from being binding on the survivor. The court is not in a position to assess the significance of the alteration to the parties, or whether it was subjectively intended to revoke the arrangement: *Re Hobley* (1997) [2006] W.T.L.R. 467.

22–34   ADD TO NOTE 63: This passage was cited with approval in *Thomas and Agnes Carvel Foundation v Carvel* [2007] EWHC 1314 (Ch), [2008] Ch. 395.

22–36   ADD FOOTNOTE AFTER THE SECOND SENTENCE: *Thomas and Agnes Carvel Foundation v Carvel* [2007] EWHC 1314 (Ch), [2008] Ch. 395 at [27] *per* Lewison J.

AMEND THE SECOND PARAGRAPH TO READ: The doctrine of mutual wills survives from the period before the full development of the doctrine of privity of contract. The basis of the trust is the express agreement between the testators. The trust gives effect to the beneficary's equitable right to compel the the benefit of obligations binding on the surviving testator's conscience. It does not depend on the beneficiary's having any contractual entitlement to compel specific performance of the agreement: *Olins v Walters* [2009] EWCA 782, [2009] Ch. 212 at [36] *per* Mummery L.J. Hence it is no objection that the beneficiary was not a party to the agreement, and that damages might have been an adequate remedy for the survivor's breach of it.

The explanation of the doctrine is similar to that of secret trusts. The first testator is treated as having made a disposition of property in reliance upon the survivor carrying out his obligations under it. It would be a fraud for the survivor to resile from it.

22–37   ADD AT BEGINNING OF PARAGRAPH:

6. Constructive Trusts of Land to Enforce an Informal Common Intention

1. General

NOTE: All of Part 6 of the main work now needs to be read in the light of the decision of the House of Lords in *Stack v Dowden* [2007] UKHL 17, [2007] 2 A.C. 432. It redefines the approach to finding that a constructive trust has arisen to enforce an an informal common intention as to the beneficial ownership of land, and to quantifying the parties' beneficial shares under it.

The main elements of the decision are described in the additions to the existing text of the main work. For the sake of clarity they are summarised together here.

Stack v Dowden re-affirms the primary importance of any declaration of express trust in determining the nature and extent of the parties' beneficial interests in the land. An express declaration of trust is conclusive unless varied by subsequent agreement or affected by proprietary estoppel: *ibid.* at [49] *per* Baroness Hale.

A declaration in the conveyance to the joint registered proprietor of the land that the survivor of them can give a valid receipt for capital money arising on a disposition of the land is not of itself a declaration of an express trust creating a beneficial joint tenancy: *ibid,* at [51] *per* Baroness Hale, [130] *per* Lord Neuberger.

In the absence of an express trust defining the beneficial ownership of the property, then, as a starting point, the court will infer that the parties intended the beneficial ownership of the property to follow the registered legal proprietorship of it. If the property is registered in the name of a sole legal proprietor, it will be inferred that he is also the sole beneficial owner. If it is registered at law in the names of joint legal proprietors, it will be inferred that they hold for themselves as joint beneficial tenants in equity: *ibid.,* at [4] *per* Lord Walker, [56] *per* Baroness Hale, [109] *per* Lord Neuberger.

A party who alleges that this *prima facie* inference does not reflect the parties' intentions bears the burden of proving that it should be displaced: *ibid.,* at [14] *per* Lord Walker, [56] *per* Baroness Hale. The burden is a heavy one: *ibid.,* at [68] *per* Baroness Hale.

The consequence of this *prima facie* inference is that a joint legal proprietor who could not prove an express agreement that she should take a beneficial share in the property and who did not make any direct financial contribution to purchasing it, would nonetheless be assumed to have a beneficial interest in the property: *ibid.,* at [63] *per* Baroness Hale.

The approach described in paragraphs 22–40—22–41 and 22–43 of the main work to proving whether a party has a beneficial interest in the property would now apply mainly to cases of sole legal proprietorship, and not to joint legal proprietorship.

In the case of a sole legal proprietor (where there is a *prima facie* inference that he is also the sole beneficial owner), the court may now infer a common intention that the beneficial ownership was to be shared with the claimant from a range of evidence that goes beyond a direct money contribution by her to purchasing the property or from the fact that she has contributed to paying mortgage instalments on it. The approach taken in *Lloyd's Bank plc v Rosset* [1991] 1 A.C. 107, 133B is perhaps too restrictive: [2007] UKHL 17, [2007] 2 A.C. 432, at [26] *per* Lord Walker, [63] *per* Baroness Hale. If the claimant incurs substantial capital expenditure on making significant improvements to the property that may perhaps justify the inference that it was agreed that she should take a beneficial interest in it: *cf. ibid.,* at [139] *per* Lord Neuberger.

When the court comes to quantify each party's beneficial share under the trust, its aim is to draw an objective inference as to their actual intentions, in the light of their actions and statements. The court's view of fairness is not the correct yardstick for determining the parties' shares: *ibid.,* at [125]–[127] *per* Lord Neuberger. In drawing the inference, many more facts than financial contributions may be relevant. As an indicative guide, they may include: advice or discussions at the time of the transfer; the reasons why the home was acquired in joint or sole names; the purpose for which the home was acquired; the nature of the parties' relationship; how the purchase was financed; how the parties arranged their finances; and how they discharged their outgoings on the property and other expenses: *ibid.*, at [69] *per* Baroness Hale. Evidence about the parties' dealings with each other after they acquire the property should not be taken into account if it does not cast light on their intentions about the beneficial ownership of the property: *Holman v Howes* [2007] EWCA Civ 877, (2007) 10 ITELR 492.

REPLACE PART OF THIRD PARAGRAPH WITH THE FOLLOWING: The rules about constructive trusts must be put in their proper context. First, they overlap to some extent with the presumptions of intention about the transfer of money or property that give rise to a resulting trust. (See Ch. 23) A person who has made a financial contribution to the purchase of property in the name of another may, depending on the context, take a beneficial interest either under a resulting trust or under a constructive trust. But differences exist between the conditions for proof of the two trusts. A direct financial contribution is not always necessary to establish an interest under a constructive trust; and different rules apply to quantifying the extent of the parties' beneficial interests in the property under the two kinds of trust. Indeed, it is nowadays less likely that a presumption of resulting trust would be applied in a dispute over the beneficial ownership of a family home. Resulting trust reasoning would, however, remain relevant in determining the beneficial shares in a commercial property: *Stack v Dowden* [2007] UKHL 17, [2007] 2 A.C. 432, at [3] *per* Lord Hope, [42] *per* Baroness Hale.

22–38   ADD TO FOOTNOTE 78: *Stack v Dowden* [2007] UKHL 17, [2007] 2 A.C.432.

ADD TO FOOTNOTE 79: A declaration in the conveyance that the survivor of two joint registered proprietors may give a valid receipt for the proceeds of sale of the property does not of itself amount to an express declaration of a beneficial joint tenancy: *Stack v Dowden* [2007] UKHL 17, [2007] 2 A.C. 432.

ADD TO FOOTNOTE 80: *Stack v Dowden* [2007] UKHL 17, [2007] 2 A.C. 432, at [66] *per* Baroness Hale. Since 1998 the Land Registry standard transfer form has provided a box for the transferees to declare the trusts on which the registered legal estate is held.

22–40   ADD TO FOOTNOTE 89: The relevant intention should be found when the property was acquired, though later conduct may be relevant to proving what was previously intended: *Supperstone v Hurst* [2005] EWHC 1309 (Ch), [2005] BPIR 1231, [2005] 25 E.G. 192 (C.S.).

ADD AFTER FIRST SENTENCE: In the absence of an express trust defining the beneficial ownership of the property, then, as a starting point, the court will infer that the parties intended the beneficial ownership of the property to follow the registered legal proprietorship of it. If the property is registered in the name of a sole legal proprietor, it will be inferred that he is also the sole beneficial owner. If it is registered at law in joint names, it will be inferred that they hold for themselves as joint beneficial tenants in equity: [2007] UKHL 17, [2007] 2 A.C. 432, at [4] *per* Lord Walker, [56] *per* Baroness Hale, [109] *per* Lord Neuberger. A party who alleges that this *prima facie* inference does not reflect the parties' intentions bears the burden of proving that it should be displaced: *ibid.*, at [14] *per* Lord Walker, [56] *per* Baroness Hale. The burden is a heavy one: *ibid.*, at [68] *per* Baroness Hale. The presumption of joint beneficial ownership from joint legal proprietorship may be more easily rebutted where the parties buy the property as an investment rather than as a shared home: *Laskar v Laskar* [2008] EWCA Civ 347, [2008] 1 W.L.R. 2695.

ADD TO FOOTNOTE 97: The logic of these findings has been questioned. It is thought that an unwarranted excuse might better found an estoppel than provide evidence of an agreement that the claimant should take an interest in the property: *Van Laethem v Brooker* [2005] EWHC 1478 (Ch), [2006] 2 F.L.R. 495 at [67] *per* Lawrence Collins J.

ADD TO PARAGRAPH HEADED "CONDUCT": The conduct relied upon must at least be known to the party who holds the legal estate. Otherwise it cannot support an inference of an agreement between them: *Lightfoot v Lightfoot-Brown* [2005] EWCA Civ 201; [2005] W.T.L.R. 1031. Similarly, one party's undisclosed intentions about the beneficial interest in the property cannot be relied upon as evidence for inferring what the two parties' shared intentions might have been: *Fowler v Barron* [2008] EWCA Civ 377, [2008] W.T.L.R. 819.

ADD AFTER SENTENCE ACCOMPANYING FOOTNOTE 5: But inthe case of a sole legal proprietor (where there is now a *prima facie* inference that he is the sole beneficial owner), the court may infer a common intention that the beneficial ownership was to be shared with the claimant from a range of evidence that goes beyond a direct money contribution by her to purchasing the property or from the fact that she has contributed to paying mortgage instalments on it. Nowadays, the narrow approach taken in the quotation is perhaps regarded as too restrictive: *Stack v Dowden* [2007] UKHL 17, [2007] 2 A.C. 432, at [26] *per* Lord Walker, [63] *per* Baroness Hale. If the claimant incurs substantial capital expenditure on making significant improvements to the property, that may some-times justify the inference that it was agreed that she should take a beneficial interest in it: *cf. ibid.*, at [139] *per* Lord Neuberger.

ADD AFTER TEXT ACCOMPANYING FOOTNOTE 10: The critical point is that the **22–41** claimant incurs the detriment in reliance on the common intention. It is unnecessary that defendant should have bargained for the detriment to be incurred: *Parris v Williams* [2008] EWCA Civ 1147, [2009] B.P.I.R. 96

REPLACE WHOLE PARAGRAPH WITH THE FOLLOWING: **22–42**

(c) Nature and extent of interest. Once it is established that the claimant has some interest in the property, its nature and extent must be

determined. [See generally *Oxley v Hiscock* [2004] EWCA Civ 546; [2005] Fam. 211; *Stack v Dowden* [2007] UKHL 17, [2007] 2 A.C. 432.] In principle, the question depends on inferences drawn by the court as to what was agreed between the parties, and, as a starting point, the court will infer that they intended their beneficial interests in the property to follow the registered legal estate. [See para. 22–40 above] Where the claimant contends that she has a different beneficial interest in the property, the court seeks to draw an objective inference as to the parties' actual intentions, in the light of their actions and statements. The court's view of fairness is not the correct yardstick for determining the parties' shares. But a clearly unjust result may justify the court in revisting its reasoning in inferring the parties' intention: *Stack v Dowden* [2007] UKHL 17, [2007] 2 A.C. 432, at [125]–[127] *per* Lord Neuberger; *Laskar v Laskar* [2008] EWCA Civ 347, [2008] 1 W.L.R. 2695 at [33].

Occasionally, the proper inference will be that the parties intended that they should have successive interests in the property. [*Ungarian v Lesnoff* [1990] Ch. 206; *Pritchard Englefield v Steinberg* [2004] EWHC 1908 (Ch); [2005] 1 P.& C.R. D6] Usually, however, the inference is that both take immediate beneficial interests as co-owners.

The court is not limited to examining the direct contributions made by the parties to the purchase price. As an indicative guide, relevant factors may include: advice or discussions at the time of the transfer; the reasons why the home was acquired in joint or sole names; the purpose for which the home was acquired; the nature of the parties' relationship; how the purchase was financed; how the parties arranged their finances; and how they discharged their outgoings on the property and other expenses: [2007] UKHL 17, [2007] 2 A.C. 432, at [69] *per* Baroness Hale. The value of the discount allowed under a tenant's right to buy the freehold may be taken as a monetary contribution by the tenant: *Laskar v Laskar* [2008] EWCA Civ 347, [2008] 1 W.L.R. 2695 at [22]–[26] *per* Neuberger L.J. The fact that both parties assume a joint legal liability as mortgagors is not necessarily treated as an contribution by each of them for the amount of the mortgage: *ibid.* at [27]–[31] *per* Neuberger L.J.

In the last resort, the maxim "equality is equity" [See above paras 5–20 et seq.] may need to be applied to determine what was intended by the parties. [*Rimmer v Rimmer* [1953] 1 Q.B. 63; *Fribrance v Fribrance (No 2)* [1957] 1 W.L.R. 384; *Gissing v Gissing* [1971] A.C. 886, 897, 903, 908; *Midland Bank v Cooke* [1995] 4 All E.R. 562, 574] But, realistically, the maxim may now only be relevant where the property is held by a sole legal proprietor since in cases of joint legal proprietorship, it would generally be inferred that the property was held subject to a beneficial joint tenancy. The shares once ascertained are absolute and indefeasible. [*Turton v Turton* [1988] Ch. 542, 554] They are not liable to be diminished or defeated by some subsequent event, such as the separation of the couple. In exceptional cases, however, the court might find that the parties have agreed to vary their original shares, provided that there has been detrimental reliance on that agreement in the usual way. [*Clarke v Harlowe* [2005] EWHC 3062 (Ch), [2006] B.P.I.R. 636] Consequently, the full value of the share is payable when the property is sold or otherwise realised, [*Turton v Turton* [1988] Ch. 542, disapproving *Hall v Hall* (1982) 3 F.L.R. 126; cf. *Gordon v Douce* [1983] 1 W.L.R. 563 which suggests, questionably, that the court has a discretion to order valuation at an earlier date.] subject only to such credits as may be allowed by way of equitable accounting, e.g., in respect of mortgage payments or improvements made after the parties have separated. [See below para. 18–28] In the case of successive interests, the court will order an actuarial valuation of their present value. [Pritchard Englefield v Steinberg [2004] EWHC 1908 (Ch), [2005] 1 P.& C.R. D6]

DELETE PARAGRAPH HEADED "INDIRECT CONTRIBUTIONS".   **22–43**

CHAPTER 23

RESULTING TRUSTS

ADD TO NOTES 1 & 4: Swadling (2008) 124 L.Q.R. 72.   **23–1**

ADD TO NOTE 6: It is argued that the more specific fact presumed from   **23–2**
the gratuitous transfer of property is that A intended B to hold the
property on trust for him: Swadling (2008) 124 L.Q.R. 72. The difference
is significant to the rejection of the argument that resulting trusts may
arise to reverse unjust enrichment. If the presumption were that A did
not intend B to become the beneficial owner of the property, then B
could not so easily rebut a presumption of a resulting trust over
property which had been lost by A, or stolen from him by B.

ADD AFTER SECOND PARAGRAPH: Proof by direct evidence depends on an
objective inference drawn from the words and conduct of the parties:
Gissing v Gissing [1971] A.C. 886, 906 *per* Lord Diplock.

ADD AT END OF THIRD SENTENCE: It should not lead to a conclusion which   **23–5**
is contrary to a common sense interpretation of the facts of the
transaction: *Vajpeyi v Yusaf* [2003] EWHC (Ch) 2339; [2004] W.T.L.R. 989.

ADD TO FOOTNOTE 17: And see *Ali v Khan* [2009] WTLR 157.

ADD AT END OF PARAGRAPH: It has been argued that the use of strict rules **23–10**
governing the evidence which may be admitted to support or rebut the
presumption of resulting trust should be liberalised. In principle, even
evidence of the parties' subsequent conduct should be admissible in
their own favour, since the judge would be free to assess its probative
weight. [Fung (2006) 122 L.Q.R. 651] This approach would be consistent
with the diminishing probative weight which the modern authorities
now attach to the presumption of advancement. [See para. 23–05 above]

ADD TO FOOTNOTE 97: But when only one member of a non-charitable **23–22**
unincorporated association remains, the starting point is that the assets
should belong beneficially to him and free from the contractual
restraints that bound them while the association still existed. There is no
reason of principle why they should pass as *bona vacantia*: *Hanchett-
Stamford v Attorney General* [2008] EWHC 330 (Ch), [2009] Ch. 173.

ADD TO FOOTNOTE 6: This section was cited with approval in *Freeman v* **23–25**
Customs and Excise Commissioners [2005] EWHC (Ch) 582; [2005] 2 P. &
C.R. DG7.

REPLACE FOOTNOTE 8 WITH THE FOLLOWING: For possible variations in
structuring the transaction, see *Freeman v Customs and Excise Commissioners* [2005] EWHC (Ch) 582; [2005] 2 P. & C.R. DG7 at [24].

23-26   ADD AFTER TEXT ACCOMPANYING NOTE 10: The question depends on the proper construction of the parties' intentions: *Templeton Insurance Ltd v Penningtons Solicitors LLP* [2006] EWHC 685 (Ch), [2007] W.T.L.R. 1103; *Cooper v P.R.G. Powerhouse Ltd. (in liquidation)* [2008] EWHC 498 (Ch), [2008] B.P.I.R. 492, [2009] 1 All E.R. (Comm.) 964.

ADD TO NOTE 10: It is not fatal to finding the required intention that A comtemplates that the money may be mingled with B's general funds: *Cooper v P.R.G. Powerhouse Ltd. (in liquidation)* [2008] EWHC 498 (Ch), [2008] B.P.I.R. 492, [2009] 1 All E.R. (Comm.) 964. But a requirement that the money is to be kept unmixed in a special account strengthens the inference that B does not have it at his free disposal, and that he is not a simple contract debtor: *Re Farepak Food and Gifts Ltd (in administration)* [2006] EWHC 3272 (Ch), [2008] B.C.C. 22.

CHAPTER 24

TRUSTS ARISING FROM WRONGS

ADD TO FOOTNOTE 5: *Yeoman's Row Management Ltd v Cobbe* [2008] UKHL **24–2**
55 at [17], [30] *per* Lord Scott.

ADD AT END OF FOOTNOTE 34: *Shalson v Russo* [2003] EWHC 1637 (Ch); **24–8**
[2005] Ch. 281 at [115] *per* Rimer J.

ADD AT END OF FOOTNOTE 37: As a justification for treating the defendant
as a constructive trustee, the force of this reason has been questioned:
Shalson v Russo [2003] EWHC 1637 (Ch); [2005] Ch. 281 at [110] *per*
Rimer J.

ADD AT END OF FOOTNOTE 39: *Shalson v Russo* [2003] EWHC 1637 (Ch);
[2005] Ch. 281 at [106]–[127] per Rimer J

ADD TO FOOTNOTE 43: *Daraydan Holdings Ltd v Solland International Ltd*
[2004] EWHC 622 (Ch); [2005] 4 All E.R. 73 at [88] *per* Lawrence Collins
J.

ADD TO FOOTNOTE 47: *Fortex Group Ltd. v Macintosh* [1998] 3 N.Z.L.R. 171 **24–9**
at 175 per Tipping J.

ADD TO FOOTNOTE 53: *Sinclair Investment Holdings SA v Versailles Trade
Finance Ltd* [2005] EWCA Civ 722; [2006] 1 B.C.L.C. 78. Despite these
indications, the recognition of a remedial constructive seems very
unlikely. The fact that the defendant's behaviour is unconscionable in
some general sense is not a sufficient reason for imposing a constructive
trust on his property. His conduct must be of a type where the courts
have recognised a constructive trust as a matter of authority: *Yeoman's
Row Management Ltd v Cobbe* [2008] UKHL 55 at [37] *per* Lord Scott.

CHAPTER 25

APPOINTMENT, RETIREMENT AND REMOVAL OF TRUSTEES

NOTE 35. ADD: *Re Papadimitriou* [2004] W.T.L.R. 1141 (Isle of Man). **25–11**

ADD TO NOTE 82: For this purpose, an "indvidual" means a natural **25–12** person and does not include a corporation: *Jasmine Trustees Ltd v Wells & Hind (a firm)* [2007] EWHC 238 (Ch), [2007] W.T.L.R. 489.

ADD AT END OF FOOTNOTE 80: Considered in *Jasmine Trustees v Wells & Hind* [2007] 3 W.L.R. 810.

ADD TO FOOTNOTE 95. In *Bridge Trustees Ltd v Noel Penny* 2008 P.L.R. 345 **25–14** it was held that this power can only be used to appoint a trustee properly so called, and this does not include an independent trustee under a pension scheme, albeit that the court might appoint him under its inherent power (in that case for the purpose of distributing surplus assets).

NOTE 60. ADD: For the situation where the terms of a trust allow the **25–26** trustee to resign, see *Custodial Ltd v Cardinal Financial Services Ltd* (2005) 7 I.T.E.L.R. 512

Chapter 26

THE POWERS OF TRUSTEES

ADD TO FOOTNOTE 16. And see Ferris and Battersby (2009) Conv 39. **26–3**

ADD TO FOOTNOTE 16. And see Ferris and Battersby (2009) Conv 39. **26–3**

7 Maintenance and Advancement

1. Express powers

(b) Advancement

NOTE 63. ADD: *Re Clore's S.T.* was applied in *X v A* [2006] 1 W.L.R. 741, **26–36**
and in *Farnsworth v Leigh* [2006] W.T.L.R. 477.

3. Statutory power of advancement

NOTE 33. ADD: *Pilkington v IRC* was considered in *Re Pinto's Settlement* **26–47**
[2004] W.T.L.R. 879 (Jersey).

CHAPTER 27

THE DUTIES AND DISCRETIONS OF TRUSTEES

2. Duties and discretions

NOTE 4. ADD: *Wendt v Orr* [2005] W.T.L.R. 223 (Western Australia).   **27-2**

AFTER *Abacus v NSPCC* [2001] S.T.C. ADD: *Hearn v Younger* [2005] P.L.R. 49; *Gallaher Ltd v Gallaher Pensions Ltd* [2005] P.L.R. 103; *Betaforce v Veys* [2006] W.T.L.R. 941.

NOTE 15. For a thorough analysis of the *Re Hastings - Bass* principle, see *Burrell v Burrell* [2005] Pen L.R. 289 where a deed of appointment entered into without regard to adverse tax consequences was avoided. In so far as there was any additional requirement for a breach of duty or default on the part of the trustee or its agents or advisers, such was in any event established on the facts of that case. See also *Wu* [2007] 21 T.L.I. 62.

NOTE 17: ADD: And see *Sieff v Fox* [2005] EWHC 1312 (Ch) where it was held that only in a case where the beneficiary is entitled to require the trustees to act should it suffice to vitiate the trustees' decision to show that they might have acted differently. There (at para 119) the court also set out a helpful summary of the *Re Hastings-Bass* principle. For articles on *Sieff v Fox* see Thomas and Dowrick [2006] Conv 91, Thomas (2005) JITCP 225, Nolan and Conaglen [2006] CLJ515, Taube [2006] PCB 155. *Sieff v Fox* [2005] EWCH 1312 (Ch) has itself been considered further. In *Smithson v Hamilton* [2008] 1 W.L.R. 1453 it was held that the *Hastings Bass* principle cannot be used to change something which the trustees have done, but can only be used to set it aside altogether, and it can only apply where the relevant actions are those of the trustees, and not those, as it was in that case, of a principal employer. In *Ogden v Trustees of RSH Griffiths 2003 Settlement* [2008] WTLR 685 the court considered, and applied, the causal requirements of the principle. In *Re Griffiths (decd)* [2008] 2 All E.R. 654 the court made obiter reference (at paragraph 31) to the issue of whether the exercise of a discretion by trustees, which was vitiated by the principle, was void or voidable (but that was a case where the wider jurisdiction to relieve from a mistake was engaged). And see further (2008) 15 Int Trust Corp Planning 1 (Weaver) ("Trusts and mistakes").

3   DUTY TO KEEP ACCOUNTS AND RECORDS AND DISCLOSURE OF TRUST DOCUMENTS

1.   The duty

27–20   NOTE 26. ADD *James v Newington* [2004] W.T.L.R. 863 (Jersey).

2.   Disclosure of trust documents

27–21   NOTE 29. ADD: *Brovere v Mourant & Co (Trustees) Ltd* [2004] W.T.L.R. 1417 (Jersey). *Re the Internine Trust and intertraders Trust* (2004) 7 I.T.E.L.R. 308 (Jersey). For the position in New Zealand, see [2005] Conv. 93.; and for an application of the principle there see *Foreman v Kingstone* [2005] W.T.L.R. 823. In New Zealand it has been held that the likelihood of acrimony within the family is not of itself a reason for denying beneficiaries information to which they are entitled, and indeed the denial of information may cause or exacerbate friction: *Foreman v Kingstone* [2005] W.T.L.R. 823.

In Australia, in the context of a superannuation fund, it has been held that actuarial reports would fall within the class of documents to which a beneficiary would normally be provided access: *Crowe v Stevedoring Employees Retirement Fund Pty Ltd* [2005] W.T.L.R. 1271.

In *Breakspear v Ackland* [2008] WTLR 777, where there was a survey of the relevant authorities, it was held that the confidence ordinarily attached to a letter of wishes was such that, for the better discharge of their functions, trustees need not disclose it to beneficiaries merely because it is requested, unless in their view disclosure is in the interests of the administration of the trust, and the discharge of their powers and discretions. For a note, see [2008] C.L.J. (Fox).

4   CONTROL BY BENEFICIARIES

2.   Rule in *Saunders v Vautier*

27–25   NOTE 52. ADD: For an article see Matthews (2006) 122 L.Q.R. 266.

ADD NEW PARAGRAPH AT END OF SECTION: In principle, the rule in *Saunders v Vautier* may apply as much to trusts in a commercial setting as to traditional family trusts. But it should not be applied where it would undermine the fundamental commercial purpose of the transaction in which the trust device has been used. For example, the rule would not entitle the beneficiaries of a pension trust to wind up the scheme and require the trustees to pay out the scheme assets, if that would circumvent any statutory rules regulating the winding up of the scheme and frustrate the employer's purpose in providing periodic benefits during the members' retirement. [*Rogers Communications Inc v Buschau* (2006) 269 D.L.R. (4th) 1] But it would not necessarily prevent an entire class of bondholders from terminating the trust on which the bonds were held and requiring payment of the bonds directly to themselves.

[*Law Debenture Trust Corporation v Elektrim Finance NV* [2006] EWHC 1305 (Ch)]

NOTE 86. AFTER *Oke v Rideout* [1998] 10 CL 559: ADD: *W v W* [2004]2 **27–32** F.L.R. 321, [2003] EWCA Civ 924. In the latter case it was held that where there was a potential application under both the 1996 Act and the Children Act 1989 ordinarily an application should be brought under both Acts.

ADD AT END OF NOTE 87: A party may be estopped from seeking an immediate order for sale: *Holman v Howes* [2007] B.P.I.R. 1085.

NOTE 88. ADD: *Olszanecki v Hillocks* [2004] W.T.L.R. 975.

NOTE 88. AFTER *Bank of Ireland Home Mortgages v Bell* [2001] B.P.I.R. 429, ADD: *Edwards v Lloyds TSB Bank Plc* [2004] B.P.I.R. 1190, [2004] EWHC 1745 (Ch). For an article on these provisions, see Pascoe [2000] Conv 54.

NOTE 90. ADD: *Dean v Stout* [2005] B.P.I.R. 1113. In *Avis v Turner* [2008] Ch 218 it was held that a trustee in bankruptcy of a husband could seek an order for sale notwithstanding the existence of a pre-existing property adjustment order made in matrimonial proceedings.

5   CONTROL BY COURT

3.   Departure from the terms of the trust

(e)   Variation of Trusts Act 1958

NOTE 90. AFTER *Allen v Distillers Company (Biochemicals) Ltd* [1974] QB 383 **27–40** ADD: (distinguished in *CD v O* [2004] W.T.L.R. 751, [2004] 3 All E.R. 780, [2004] EWHC 1036 (Ch).)

CHAPTER 28

BREACH OF TRUST

2 REMEDIES AGAINST THE TRUSTEE

10. Defences

(b) Exemption clauses

REPLACE NOTE 16 WITH THE FOLLOWING: Law Commission, *Trustee Exemption* **28–26**
Clauses (Law Com. No 301).

REPLACE TEXT ACCOMPANYING NOTE 19 WITH THE FOLLOWING: Such clauses
are construed fairly according to the natural meaning of the words used,
without any presumption against the interests of the trustee. But kinds
of liability which are not clearly covered by the terms of the exclusion
clause should be treated as falling outside it. [*Bogg v Raper, The Times*,
April 22, 1998].

ADD TO NOTE 20: A trustee who believes her acts are morally justified,
or that her actions have not fallen below acceptable standards, may
nonetheless be held to have acted dishonestly if an ordinary, honest
trustee would not have acted as she did: *Wong v Burt* [2004] NZCA 174;
[2005] W.T.L.R. 29; *Barnes v Tomlinson* [2006] EWHC 3115, [2007]
W.T.L.R. 377. See also on *Armitage v Nurse: Baker v J E Clark & Co
(Transport) Ltd* [2006] Pens L.R. 131.

(c) Lapse of time

(1) THE PERIOD

DELETE TEXT ACCOMPANYING NOTE 32   **28–27**

ADD NEW PARAGRAPH TO SECTION HEADED ''(3) EXCEPTIONS'':
There is an important qualification to what is meant by a '' trustee'' from
whom the claimant seeks to recover the trust property or its proceeds. It
does not apply to a person who becomes a so-called ''constructive
trustee'' merely because he is liable to account for his fraud or some
other breach of equitable duty. So a defendant who is liable as a
constructive trustee for dishonest assistance in another person's breach
of trust does not remain indefinitely liable to the claimant. It makes no
difference whether the primary breach of trust was committed fraudulently or not. He can take advantage of the general limitation period,
which is typically six years. [*Cattley v Pollard* [2006] EWHC 3130 (Ch),

[2007] 2 All E.R. 1086; but cf *Statek Corporation v Alford* [2008] EWHC 32 (Ch), [2008] B.C.C. 266 where it was said, *obiter*, that liability for dishonest assistance should not be subject to a limitation period, at least perhaps where the primary breach of trust was committed fraudulently. See Mitchell [2008] Conv 226.] The kind of trustee whose liability remains indefinite is one who held the relevant property *qua* trustee before he committed the breach of legal duty for which the claimant sues. The trustee's liability is indefinite since he is treated as having possession of the property on the beneficiary's behalf both before and after he commits the breach of trust. [*Paragon Finance v D.B. Thakerer & Co Ltd* [1999] 1 All E.R. 400; *Halton International Holdings SARL v Guernoy Ltd* [2006] EWCA Civ 801.]

ADD AFTER TEXT ACCOMPANYING NOTE 52: The beneficiary cannot be expected to risk litigation in respect of damage to a future interest which he may never live to enjoy. [*Cattley v Pollard* [2006] EWHC 3130 (Ch), [2007] 2 All E.R. 1086] The possibility of a beneficary having property appointed to him under a discretionary trust does not postpone the running of time until he in fact receives the property. He has until then no future interest in the trust. If, however, his right is under a contingent interest, time will not run against him until the interest vests. [*Johns v Johns* [2004] NZCA 42; [2005] W.T.L.R. 529.]

ADD TO NOTE 32: The defence of laches remains available even though the trustee's liability is not subject to any statutory period of limitation: *Re Loftus (deceased)* [2006] EWCA Civ 1124, [2007] 1 W.L.R. 591.

ADD TO NOTE 54: *Paragon Finance v D.B. Thakerer & Co Ltd* [1999] 1 All E.R. 400, 418 *per* Millett L.J.

3   PROPRIETARY CLAIMS ARISING FROM A BREACH OF TRUST

3.   Following and tracing in equity

(a)   Equitable title to trace

28–35   ADD AT END OF SECOND PARAGRAPH: The claimant's equitable title need not give him a beneficial interest in the property. It would be enough, for example, that he had an equitable charge over the original asset: *Dick v Harper* (2001) [2006] B.P.I.R. 20.

(c)   Tracing into a mixed fund comprising contributions of the beneficiary and an innocent volunteer

28–39   INSERT AT END OF NOTE 30: It has even been held that the rule in *Clayton's Case* can be displaced where it would be unjust or impractical to apply it, regardless of the intentions of the contributors: *Commerzbank A.G. v IMB Morgan Plc* [2004] EWHC 2771 (Ch); [2005] 2 All E.R. (Comm.) 564; [2005] 1 Lloyd's L.R. 298. In the absence of evidence of the relative amount of the claimants' contributions, the mixed fund should, in principle, be divided among them equally: *Re French Caledonia Travel* (2004) 22 A.C.L.C. 498, noted [2005] C.L.J. 45.

4. Loss of right to trace or follow; defences to claims based on following and tracing

(a) Dissipation and failure of identification

ADD TO NOTE 33: *Re Goldcorp Exchange Ltd* [1995] 1 A.C. 74 at 104–105; **28–41** *Shalson v Russo* [2003] EWHC 1637; [2005] Ch. 281, at [140] per Rimer J.

4 PERSONAL LIABILITY OF THIRD PARTIES INVOLVED IN A BREACH OF TRUST

ADD AT END OF SECOND PARAGRAPH: All these claims brought against third **28–45** parties have the effect of reducing the amount of the beneficiary's loss resulting from the breach of trust. Any sum which the beneficiary recovers would therefore be reflected in a reduction of the amount of the trustee's primary liability for the breach. Equally, a third party who is liable to give restitution of money which he received beneficially, and with unconscionable knowledge that it derived from the breach, may claim a contribution from other parties who are liable in respect of the same damage. For the purposes of the contribution, the claim against the beneficial recipient is treated as one to recover compensation for damage sustained through the initial breach [*Charter Plc v City Index Ltd* [2007] EWCA Civ 1382, [2008] Ch. 313, applying Civil Liability (Contribution) Act 1978, s.6(1)].

ADD FOOTNOTE TO FIRST PARAGRAPH OF SECTION 28–46: **28–46**

(a) *Claims based on receipt of or dealing with trust money* This passage was cited with approval in *Uzinterimpex J.S.C. v Standard Bank Plc* [2008] EWCA Civ 819.

ADD TO NOTE 44: In Australia the requirement of the defendant's fault has been affirmed. The argument that the defendant's liability should be strict, and explained on a principle of preventing unjust enrichment, has been specifically rejected: *Farah Constructions Pty Ltd v Say-Dee Pty Ltd* [2007] HCA 22; noted Conaglen and Nolan [2007] C.L.J. 515, Ridge and Dietrich (2008) 124 L.Q.R. 26.

REPLACE FINAL SECTION OF PARAGRAPH WITH THE FOLLOWING:

(3) DISHONEST ASSISTANCE IN BREACH OF TRUST.

(See generally Mitchell, Ch. 6 in Birks and Pretto (eds), *Breach of Trust* (2002)).

A person who dishonestly assists a trustee in committing a breach of his duty may be liable to the beneficiary. (The principle is not confined to breaches of trust but extends to breaches by other fiduciaries, such as the duties owed by partners in a fiduciary joint venture (*Abou-Rahmah v Abacha* [2005] EWHC 2662 (QB), [2006] Lloyd's Rep 484 at [38]) and that owed by a director to his company: *Baden v Societe Generale* [1993] 1 W.L.R. 509 at 573; but see *Brown v Bennett* [1999] B.C.C. 525, *Goose v Wilson Sandford & Co* [2001] Lloyd's Rep. PN 189 and *Gencor ACP Ltd v Dalby* [2002] 2 B.C.L.C. 734 at 757 where the point was left open.) His liability is based on his being an accessory to the trustee's wrong and does not depend on his having received any trust property. It is not necessary that the primary breach of trust committed should be dishonest or fraudulent (*Royal Brunei Airlines Sdn Bhd v Tan* [1995] 2 A.C. 378).

The defendant must be proved to have been dishonest in giving his assistance to the trustee's breach. In applying this standard, it is clear that the defendant is not free to be judged according to his own standards of honesty. He is judged according the standard of ordinary honest people (*Royal Brunei Airlines Sdn Bhd v Tan* [1995] 2 A.C. 378). The authorities have in the past been uncertain about whether the trustee also needs to be aware that his conduct would be regarded as dishonest by this standard. The better view, which now appears to be accepted in England, is that it is unnecessary for the defendant to take a view on the propriety of his conduct. (Compare *Twinsectra Ltd v Yardley* [2002] 2 A.C. 164; [2002] UKHL 165 at [32]–[35] with *Barlow Clowes v Eurotrust International Ltd* [2005] UKPC 37;[2006] 1 All E.R. 333 at [15]–[16]. In *Abou-Rahmah v Abacha* [2006] EWCA Civ 1492, [2007] W.T.L.R. 1, where this passage was cited with approval, Arden L.J. held that the later decision of the Privy Council in the Barlow Clowes case represented the correct interpretation of English law). A finding that the defendant was dishonest need only involve an assessment of his participation in the light of his knowledge of the facts of the transaction.

The finding of the defendant's dishonesty will depend on how precisely he knew the facts which amounted to the breach of trust, and the extent to which his assistance in the transaction involved a commercially unacceptable risk of knowingly implicating himself in the trustee's wrongful conduct. For this purpose, knowledge and a deliberate choice by the defendant not to confirm his suspicions are treated alike (*Attorney General of Zambia v Meer Care & Desai (a firm)* [2008] EWCA Civ 1007 at [21] per Lloyd L.J.) A negligent or incompetent failure to realise the unlawfulness of the transaction that he assists is not enough (*Royal Brunei Airlines Sdn Bhd v Tan* [1995] 2 A.C. 378, 391–392 *per* Lord Nicholls).

It is not necessary that the defendant should appreciate the precise legal significance of the transaction as amounting to a breach of trust. It is enough that he realises that the person whom he assists is misappropriating money over which he does not have a right of free disposal (*Twinsectra Ltd v Yardley* [2002] UKHL 165; [2002] 2 A.C. 164 at [137] *per* Lord Millett; *Barlow Clowes v Eurotrust International Ltd* [2005] UKPC 37,

[2006] 1 All E.R. 333 at [28] per Lord Hoffmann). But he must have some suspicions about the particular transactions to which he gives his assistance. A general suspicion, for example, that the transaction is of a kind which was consistent with the possibility of money laundering would not be sufficiently direct to be dishonest (*Abou-Rahmah v Abacha* [2006] EWCA Civ 1492 at [72] *per* Arden L.J.; [98] *per* Pill L.J.).

If the defendant is proved liable, then he may be required to compensate the trust for losses following from his assistance (*Royal Brunei Airlines Sdn Bhd v Tan* [1995] 2 A.C. 378) or, possibly, to account for profits which accrue to him as a result of his assistance (*Ultraframe (UK) Ltd v Fielding* [2005] EWHC 1638 (Ch), [2007] W.T.L.R. 835). These two kinds of liability follow from the premise that the defendant is held liable to account as if he were truly a trustee to the claimant. The description of the defendant as a "constructive trustee" is simply a "formula for equitable relief" which can be recovered from him as a result of his wrongdoing (*Selangor United Rubber Estates Ltd v Cradock* [1968] 1 W.L.R. 1555 at 1582 per Ungoed-Thomas J.; *Dubai Aluminium Co Ltd v Salaam* [2002] UKHL 48; [2003] 2 A.C. 366 at [141]–[143] per Lord Millett who criticises the description of the defendant as "accountable as a constructive trustee", it being more accurate simply to describe the defendant "as accountable in equity"; see para 19–02 above.).

In relation to losses, once it is proved that the defendant has provided the relevant assistance to the breach of duty, he will be liable for losses resulting from the trustee's breach. Proof of the specific causal connection between the assistance and the loss is not necessary (*Grupo Torras SA v Al Sabah* [1999] C.L.C. 1,469 (reversed in part on appeal without comment on this point: [2001] C.L.C. 221). *Cf. Edgington v Fitzmaurice* (1885) L.R. 29 Ch.D. 459; *Banque Bruxelles Lambert SA v Eagle Star Insurance Co Ltd* [1997] A.C. 191), though no doubt the defendant's act would not amount to assistance unless it had some causative effect (*Brown v Bennet* [1999] B.C.C. 525). The measure of the defendant's liability will not be reduced by reason of any contributory negligence on the part of the claimant (*Corp del Cobre de Chile v Sogemin Ltd* [1997] 1 W.L.R. 1396; *Standard Chartered Bank v Pakistan National Insurance Corp (Nos 2 and 4)* [2002] UKHL 43; [2003] 1 A.C. 959).

In relation to profits, the existence and nature of the defendant's liability remain uncertain. It seems clear, at least, that the defendant should not be required to hold a profit resulting from his wrongful assistance on a constructive trust, enforceable by a proprietary remedy, unless perhaps it accrued to him through use of the claimant's own property. (*Sinclair Investment Holdings SA v Versailles Trade Finance Ltd* [2007] EWHC 916 (Ch), [2007] 2 All E.R. (Comm.) 993) But in principle this limitation should not preclude a personal liability to account for a profit, provided that the claimant proved a sufficiently direct causal connection between the defendant's assistance and the alleged profit. On this view, the defendant should be only accountable for profits which he has made personally as a result of his assistance (*Fyffes Group v Templeman* [2002] Lloyds LR 643). He would not be accountable for profits made directly by the defaulting trustee whom he assists, unless perhaps he were entitled to receive those profits himself but diverted them to the trustee (*Ultraframe (U.K.) Ltd v Fielding* [2005] EWHC 1638 (Ch), [2007] W.T.L.R. 835 at [1598]–[1600]). Since he would be treated as if he were a trustee, he could only be held accountable for moneys which he in fact received to the use of the trust. To hold him liable for the profits of the trustee would be to subvert the proper basis of his accountability by imposing a penalty upon him.

PART VI

ADMINISTRATION OF ESTATES

CHAPTER 29

COLLECTION AND REALISATION OF ASSETS

3 COLLECTION OF ASSETS

NOTE 33. ADD AT END: See Vallat, [2004] P.C.B. 221.   **29–13**

5 POWERS OF PERSONAL REPRESENTATIVES

1. Introduction

ADD TO FOOTNOTE 50: For example, a person who has yet to be appointed **29–18**
an administrator generally has no right to possession of the deceased's
assets unless perhaps that would be necessary to safeguard the estate.
But an executor would have an immediate right to possession once the
testator died: *Caudle v L D Law* [2008] EWHC 374 (QB), [2008] 1 W.L.R.
1540.

CHAPTER 31

DISTRIBUTION OF ASSETS

1   TRANSFER OF PROPERTY

5.   Transfer to persons entitled

ADD NEW NOTE 45A AT END: See, e.g., *Re Clough-Taylor, Coutts & Co v Banks*   **31–9**
[2002] EWHC 2460 at para.12.

CHAPTER 32

REMEDIES

1 ADMINISTRATION BY THE COURT

4. Lapse of time

(b) Beneficiaries

ADD AFTER FIRST SENTENCE: It seems that the period would not begin to run 32–7 at least until after the grant of letters of administration, and, in the case of a residuary gift, until after the adminstrator was in a position to distribute the residuary estate: *Re Loftus (deceased)* [2006] EWCA Civ 1124, [2007] 1 W.L.R. 591 at [30] *per* Chadwick L.J.

2 SUBSTITUTION OR REMOVAL OF PERSONAL REPRESENTATIVES

ADD TO NOTE 63: For the approach of the court on such applications, see 32–11 *Perotti v Watson* [2001] EWCA Civ 116. An action to remove the administrator of an estate is not subject to the twelve-year limitiation period in Limitation Act 1980, s.22(a) but to the usual period applying to a beneficiary who seeks to bring an administration action: *Re Loftus (deceased)* [2006] EWCA Civ 1124, [2007] 1 W.L.R. 591

ADD AT THE END OF THE PARAGRAPH: Where the power under s.50 is exercised for the removal and replacement of a trustee, the criteria are similar to those applied by the court when it appoints a judicial trustee. The overriding consideration is the welfare of the beneficiaries and to ensure that the trusts are properly executed: *Thomas and Agnes Carvel Foundation v Carvel* [2007] EWHC 1314 (Ch), [2008] Ch. 395.

REPLACE WHOLE PARAGRAPH WITH THE FOLLOWING: 32–17

5 LIABILITY OF RECIPIENTS OF ASSETS

1. Personal claim

(a) The claim. An unpaid or underpaid creditor, legatee or next-of-kin 32–17 has a direct claim against those who have received assets of the

deceased to the extent to which the latter have been paid or overpaid in excess of their right. [*Ministry of Health v Simpson* [1951] A.C. 251, affirming *Re Diplock* [1948] Ch. 465, especially at 502. As to creditors, see A.E.A. 1925, s.32(2) (above, para. 29–12) and *Hunter v Young* (1879) 4 Ex.D. 256. The claim is available against the Crown: *Re Lowe's W.T.* [1973] 1 W.L.R. 882 at 887.] It matters not that they have spent the assets [*Ministry of Health v Simpson* above, at 276. But see G. H. Jones (1957) 73 L.Q.R. 48 at 61 *et seq.*], or that they were paid or overpaid through a mistake of law on the part of the personal representatives. [*Ministry of Health v Simpson* above, at 269–273.] This point was formerly of greater relevance before the abolition of the rule that an action would not lie for restitution of money paid by mistake of law. [*Kleinwort Benson Ltd v Lincoln City Council* [1999] 2 A.C. 349.] The claim is available whether or not the estate has been administered in court. [*Re Diplock* [1948] Ch. 465 at 502.]

The claim does not require proof of any knowledge or fault on the part of the recipient. It differs in this respect from the claim to recover money received by a person in breach of trust or some other fiduciary duty. There the beneficiary is required to prove that the recipient's knowledge of the facts was sufficient to make it unconscionable for him to retain the money. [See para. 28–46 above.] The claim for unconscionable receipt would not be available to an unsecured creditor of the trust since he would have no equitable interest in the trust fund to found his title to sue. These differences are explained by the distinct historical origin of the personal claim against a person receiving assets from a deceased estate. It was developed by the Court of Chancery as part of its endeavours to wrest from the spiritual courts jurisdiction over the administration of assets. [For the distinctness of the claim, see C. Harpum, Ch. 1 in P Birks (ed), *Frontiers of Liability* Vol. 1 (1994), and for its historical development, see S.J. Whittaker (1983) 4 J.L.H. 3.]

32–18   ADD NEW PARAGRAPH

32–18 *(b)* *Limits of claim.* The claim is available only if, and to the extent that, the claimant is without remedy against the wrongdoing personal representatives. [*Re Diplock* above, at 503, 504] Moreover, the claim does not exist if, at the time of payment, there was a sufficiency of assets to pay all the beneficiaries in full and the deficiency arose through some subsequent accident or *devastavit* committed by the personal representatives. [*Fenwicke v Clarke* (1862) 4 De G.F. & J. 240 and *Re Winslow* (1890) 45 Ch.D. 249 (accident); *Peterson v Peterson* (1866) L.R. 3 Eq. 111; and see *Re Lepine* [1892] 1 Ch. 210 (*devastavit*)] The claim does not carry interest. [*Re Diplock* [1948] Ch. 465 at 505, 506.]

32–19   ADD NEW PARAGRAPH

32–19 (c)   Limitation. The claim is liable to be defeated by the Limitation Act 1980. [*ibid.* at 507–516; affirmed [1951] A.C. 251 at 276, 277.] Where the claimant is a beneficiary under the will or intestacy of the deceased, he will be barred 12 years after his right to receive his share or interest accrued, *i.e.* normally one year from the death. [See above, para. 30–01 and Limitation Act 1980, s.22.] A creditor, on the other hand, must bring his action within six years from the accrual of his cause of action, or 12 years if he is a specialty or judgment creditor. [Limitation Act 1980, ss.5, 8, 24.]

ADD NEW PARAGRAPH   **32–20**

2. Proprietary claim

Legatees, devisees and next-of-kin may rely upon their limited equitable **32–20** title to trace the assets of the deceased, notwithstanding an assent or conveyance by the personal representative. [A.E.A. 1925, ss.36(9), 38; above, para. 31–14.] They may enforce proprietary claims against recipients other than bona fide purchasers without notice. [*Re Diplock* [1948] Ch. 465.] In this respect their claims are similar to those of a beneficiary under a trust. [Above, para. 28–35 *et seq.*]

PART VII

SECURITIES

CHAPTER 35

CREATION OF MORTGAGES

4   EQUITABLE MORTGAGES

3.   Informal Mortgages

ADD TO END OF PARAGRAPH: In some recent cases courts had shown **35–22** themselves willing to give legal effect to security agreements, notwithstanding a failure to comply with s.2 of the Law of Property (Miscellaneous Provisions) Act 1989, in reliance upon the doctrine of proprietary estoppel; see *Cobbe v Yeoman's Row Management Ltd* [2005] EWHC 266 (Ch) and *Kinane v Mackie-Conteh* [2005] EWCA Civ 45. The decision at first instance in *Cobbe* was upheld by the Court of Appeal, save in respect of the relief granted against the third defendant, which was set aside by the Court of Appeal; see *Cobbe v Yeoman's Row Management Ltd* [2006] EWCA Civ 1139. The House of Lords has however now overturned the decisions of the Judge at first instance and the Court of Appeal in this case, and refused to permit proprietary estoppel to be used as a means of circumventing s.2; see *Yeoman's Row Management Ltd v Cobbe* [2008] UKHL 55.

CHAPTER 36

SETTING ASIDE MORTGAGES

2   UNDUE INFLUENCE

1.   The doctrine

(c)   The burden of proof

NOTE 7. ADD: See *UCB Corporate Services Limited v Kohli* [2004] EWHC   **36–4**
1126 (Ch) for an example of a case where a claim of undue influence
failed. The Court of Appeal applied the guidance of Lord Nicholls in
Etridge No. 2 at [30] to find that Mrs Kohli had signed the guarantee in
the ordinary course of events and that the guarantee did not fall into the
class of guarantees which, failing proof to the contrary, were explicable
only on the basis that they had been procured by the exercise of undue
influence on the part of the husband.

CHAPTER 38

THE RIGHTS AND INTEREST OF THE MORTGAGEE

3   RIGHT TO POSSESSION

1.   The right to possession

ADD AT END OF FIRST PARAGRAPH: Where a party is the registered proprietor **38–10**
of a legal charge, that party retains legal ownership of the charge, and
thus the right to possession of the mortgaged property, notwithstanding
the existence of an uncompleted agreement to transfer the legal charge
to a special purpose vehicle; see *Paragon Finance Plc v Pender* [2005]
EWCA Civ 760.

5   RIGHT TO SALE OUT OF COURT

5.   Position of mortgagee on sale

NOTE 24. ADD: See also *Bradford & Bingley v Ross* [2005] EWCA where it **38–37**
was held that the failure by a building society mortgagee to disclose that
its sale of a mortgaged property was to a closely connected company
entitled the borrower to a retrial of the building society's action against
the borrower for the shortfall on the borrowing. The Court of Appeal
declined to go further and strike out the action as an abuse of process.

(b)   No trust of power

ADD AT END OF FIRST PARAGRAPH IN (B): Where the mortgaged land **38–38**
comprises a ransom strip, it has been said that the best price reasonably
obtainable on a sale by the mortgagee is not the open market value, but
is the price which can be obtained only from the person with the special
interest in purchasing; namely the owner of the ransomed land. In such
circumstances the duty of the mortgagee to secure the best price
reasonably obtainable cannot be satisfied without resort to that special
purchaser. The mortgagee is however entitled to sell at the time of its
choosing. It follows that whether the best price which is reasonably
obtainable has been achieved depends very substantially (if not entirely)
on what the special purchaser is prepared to pay at the specific time
when the mortgagee chooses to sell; see *Freeguard v Royal Bank of
Scotland Plc* [2005] EWHC 978 Ch. When exercising a power of sale it is
not necessary that the mortgagee's only motive is to recover the

mortgage debt. The power of sale may not be invalidated if the mortgagee has a mixed motive, provided that a genuine part of that motive is to recover the mortgage debt; see *Meretz Investments NV v ACP Ltd* [2006] EWHC 74 (Ch). This part of the reasoning of the Judge at first instance in this case is considered not to have been affected by the more recent decision of the Court of Appeal allowing, in part, an appeal by the claimants in this case; see *Meretz Investments NV v ACP Ltd* [2007] EWCA Civ 1303.

7   RIGHT TO APPOINT A RECEIVER

2.   Position of receiver

38–56   ADD AT END: *In OBG Ltd v Allan* [2005] EWCA Civ 106 the claimants, being companies which had gone into liquidation, brought proceedings against the defendants alleging that administrative receivers had been invalidly appointed and that they, the claimants, had suffered loss as a result of the receivers' wrongful interference with their contractual relations and conversion of their contracts. The defendants' appeal against an award of damages for wrongful interference with contractual relations was allowed by the Court of Appeal, by a majority (Mance L.J. dissenting). The intention to procure a breach of contract was an essential ingredient of the tort of wrongful interference with contractual relations. in the absence of such intention the interference by a third party with the right of a party to a contract to peform and manage the contract was not sufficient to constitute the tort. Although the receivers had intended to interfere with the claimants' business, that did not amount to interfere with contractual relations in any relevant sense.

8   LIMITATION

3.   Effects of Lapse of time

38–64   NOTE 49. DELETE REFERENCE TO S.7 AND SUBSTITUTE S.17.

ADD AT END: In *Ashe v National Westminster Bank Plc* [2008] EWCA Civ 55 the Court of Appeal had to consider the question of whether mortgagors were in adverse possession as against a mortgagee in circumstances where the mortgage lender had taken no steps to enforce its right to possession of the mortgaged property. The Court of Appeal rejected the argument of the mortgage lender that the mortgagors had been in occupation of the mortgaged property with consent of the mortgage lender, and held that the lender's charge had been extinguished pursuant to s.17 of the Limitation Act 1980.

5.   Action on the covenant

38–70   ADD AT END: In *Bradford & Bingley v Rashid* [2006] UKHL 37 the sale of the mortgaged property left a shortfall on the mortgage debt. The lender and borrower entered into negotiations over payment of the outstanding balance. When the mortgage lender eventually commenced proceedings the borrower argued that the proceedings had been commenced outside the limitation period provided by Section 20 of the Limitation Act 1980. The mortgage lender argued that the borrower's correspondence amounted to an acknowledgment of the mortgage debt which started time running afresh. The House of Lords agreed, ruling that the two relevant letters from the borrower had amounted to acknowledgments of the debt which had started time running afresh. The House of Lords accepted that without prejudice privilege could have operated to prevent the two letters from constituting such acknowledgments, but held that the two letters were not in fact subject to without prejudice privilege.

ADD AT END: in *Gotham v Doodes* [2006] EWCA Civ 1080 a trustee in bankruptcy obtained a court order imposing a charge on certain property for the benefit of the bankrupt's estate and removing the bankrupt's interest in the property from his estate, pursuant to s.313 of the Insolvency Act 1986. The court order was obtained in May 1992. In June 2004 the trustee in bankruptcy applied to the court for an order for the sale of the property. The bankrupt contended that the lapse of time between the making of the order which created the charge and the application for sale meant that the trustee was barred from recovering any sum of money secured by the charge, in reliance upon s.20(1)(a) of the Limitation Act 1980. The bankrupt's argument was that time started to run when the charge was created. The Court of Appeal held that the application for an order for sale was not time barred. The trustee's right to receive the proceeds of sale did not accrue until there was an order for sale.

NOTE 72. DELETE AND SUBSTITUTE: *West Bromwich Building Society v Wilkinson* [2005] UKHL 44. For a discussion of the decision of the House of Lords in this case, see the article in the Conveyancer, [2005] 69 Conv 469.

12   SUBROGATION

1.   Effect of subrogation

ADD AT END: A lender who obtains some security, but less than that for **38–82** which he bargained, is not precluded from claiming further security by subrogation; see *Cheltenham & Gloucester plc v Appleyard* [2004] EWCA 291. In the same case it was held, on the facts, that it was no bar to the lender raising a claim for payment and possession based upon subrogation that the lender had not raised the subrogation claim in earlier proceedings against the same borrowers in respect of the same indebtedness.

ADD AT END: For a decision on the extent of a bank's right of subrogation in relation to interest and costs see *Kali Ltd v Chawla* [2007] EWHC 1989 (Ch) [2007] EWHC 2357 (Ch)

CHAPTER 42

LIENS

1. TYPES OF LIEN

1. Legal lien

ADD AT END: In *Heath Lambert Ltd v Sociedad de Corretaje De Seguros (No. 2)* **42–2**
[2006] EWHC 1345 (Comm) an insurance broker claimed a statutory lien
over the proceeds of an insurance claim in respect of insurance
premiums for which it had not been reimbursed. The claim succeeded.
His Honour Judge Mackie QC rejected arguments that the statutory lien
had been excluded by agreement and that the statutory lien had merged
in a judgment, which the insurance broker had obtained against one of
the defendants to the claim, for the unpaid amounts in respect of the
insurance premiums. The Judge took the view both that the statutory
lien in question did not merge in the judgment, and that the position
was the same in relation to a common law lien.

2. Equitable lien

ADD AT END OF PARAGRAPH: In *Cobbe v Yeoman's Row Management Limited* **42–3**
[2005] EWHC 266 (Ch) and [2006] EWCA Civ 1139 the award of a lien to
secure an interest over certain property was the means chosen by the
Court at first instance (subsequently upheld, save in one respect, by the
Court of Appeal) to satisfy claims based upon proprietary estoppel and
constructive trust. These decisions have however now been overturned
by the House of Lords, which held that the claims based upon
proprietary estoppel and constructive trust failed, leaving the claimant
to his common law remedies in restitution; see *Yeoman's Row Management Ltd v Cobbe* [2008] UKHL 55.

2 SOLICITOR'S LIENS

2. Lien commensurate only with client's right

(c) Wairer

ADD AT END OF (c): The fact that the solicitor has no positive intention to **42–12**
waive the lien does not suffice to defeat a waiver. Where there is an

inconsistency the solicitor will be regarded as having waived the lien; see *Clifford Harris & Co v Solland International Ltd* [2005] EWHC 141 (Ch).

CHAPTER 43

SURETYSHIP

1. Definition

NOTE 5. ADD: See also *Marubeni Hong Kong and South China Ltd v* **43-2**
Mongolian Government [2005] EWCA Civ. 395 for a recent case in which
the distinction between a direct obligation to pay and a secondary or
conditional obligation to pay was considered in the context of a letter
containing a promise issued by the Government of Mongolia to pay for
certain goods. For a discussion of this case and *Triodos Bank NV v Dobbs*
[2005] EWCA Civ 630, see the article in the Law Quarterly Review,
(2006) 122 L.Q.R. January 42. See also *Pitts v Jones* [2007] EWCA Civ
1301.

1 NATURE OF SURETYSHIP

3. Creation of the obligation

ADD AT END: IN *GMAC Commercial Credit Development Ltd v Sandhu* [2004] **43-9**
EWHC 716 (Comm) it was held that Section 4 of the Statute of Frauds
1677 did not provide a valid objection to a claim for rectification of a
guarantee.

NOTE 26. ADD: In *J. Pereira Fernandes SA v Mehta* [2006] EWHC 813 (Ch)
the defendant, who was a director of a company faced with a winding
up petition, sent an e-mail to the claimant's solicitors, offering a personal
guarantee in respect of the sum owed by the company, in exchange for
the hearing of the petition being adjourned. The defendant's name did
not appear in the body of the e-mail, but his e-mail address was
automatically inserted by an internet service provider. The proposal was
orally accepted by the claimant's solicitors. The issues before the Court
were whether the e-mail was a guarantee, and whether the presence of
the defendant's e-mail address constituted a sufficient signature for the
purposes of Section 4 of the Statute of Frauds 1677. It was held that the
defendant's offer contained in the e-mail and the solicitors' oral accept-
ance was a sufficient note or memorandum for the purposes of Section
4, but that the e-mail did not contain the signature either of the
defendant or one of his authorised agents, with the result that Section 4
was not satisfied. It was held that a party could sign a document in a
number of ways, provided that the signature was inserted for the

purpose of giving authenticity to the document. The insertion of a person's e-mail address by an internet service provider after the document had been transmitted was, absent evidence to the contrary, incidental and not intended as a signature.

2   POSITION OF CREDITOR

1.   Terms of guarantee

43–11   ADD AS (C):

Non-party to a deed: In Moody v Condor Insurance Ltd [2006] EWHC 100 (Ch) it was held that the claimants who were not a party to an instrument of guarantee executed as a deed were entitled to enforce the guarantee. Park J. held that it was clear that the loan note and guarantee instrument and guarantee were the types of deed which were not merely intended to create rights enforceable by non-parties, but in law achieved that intention.

3   POSITION OF SURETY

2.   Creditor's duty not to prejudice surety

43–14   ADD AT END: A guarantor of a principal debtor's liabilities is interested in a security given for the debt, in respect of which it is a guarantor, in two respects. First, if the guarantor pays the amount owed, it is entitled to the security by way of subrogation to the rights of the creditor. Second, its liability, like that of the principal debtor, falls to be extinguished or reduced by the amount realised by the creditor on a sale of the security. It has been held that the second of these two interests does give rise to a duty on the part of the creditor, if it realises the security in respect of the liabilities of the principal debtor, to do so at a proper price; see *Barclays Bank plc v Kingston* [2006] EWHC 533 (QB).

6   DISCHARGE OF SURETY

1.   Unauthorised variation of terms

43–31   ADD AFTER FIRST SENTENCE: In *Lloyds TSB Bank plc v Hayward* [2005] EWCA Civ 466 the following statement of the rule in *Holme v Brunskill* (1878) 3 Q.B.D. 495 was approved: a guarantor is released from liability under a guarantee given to a creditor where, after the giving of the guarantee, the creditor and the principal debtor have entered into an agreement which has the effect of altering the contractual position between them to the disadvantage of the guarantor, without his prior consent; potential disadvantage is sufficient.

NOTE 92. ADD AT END: See also *ST Microelectronics NV v Condor Insurance Ltd* [2006] EWHC 977 (Comm) for a discussion of the case law in the context of a claim by a guarantor that it was released from its guarantee by virtue of what it alleged was a binding agreement between the creditor and the debtor for the debtor to pay the creditor within a time shorter than the time originally permitted by the contractual obligation which was the subject of the relevant guarantee.

ADD AT END: Where a surety guarantees that he will pay money due from the principal debtor under or pursuant to a specific loan agreement the surety cannot, without more, be required to pay sums due under subsequent agreements made between the creditor and the principal debtor, even though the surety agreement permits the creditor to agree to any amendment or variation of the loan agreement without reference to the guarantor; see *Triodos Bank NV v Dobbs* [2005] EWCA Civ 630. In *Moody v Condor Insurance Ltd* [2006] EWHC 100 (Ch) it was held that it was wrong and inconsistent with the inherent nature of a guarantee that the guarantor should be freed from liability to the third party creditor if the guarantor could establish, after the event, that he was deceived by the debtor when he agreed to give the guarantee. The guarantee in that case was held still to be enforceable by the claimants, notwithstanding that it was obtained dishonestly.

INDEX